Hannah G
x

Araceli Navarro

Big thank
to all Rock
Past and p
you're an amazing

Julie B

Marshall

L Davis

Lorraine

ANDY DUCM.

Rosy Grace

Andreea

Carly
x

Mitch Tonks

ROCKFISH
THE COOKBOOK

with recipe photography by
Chris Terry

Jon
Croft
Editions

First published in Great Britain by
Jon Croft Editions in 2021
info@joncrofteditions.com
www.joncrofteditions.com

Text © Mitch Tonks, 2021
Recipe photography © Chris Terry 2021
Photography page 103 © Ed Ovenden, 2021
Location photography © Ed Ovenden, with the
exception of pages 12–13 and 144 © Rockfish staff; page
47, top left © J. Tsang, Horizons Plymouth; pages 76–77
© Chris Terry; and pages 108–109 © Offshore Shellfish.

Page 14 © Crown Copyright and/or database rights.
Reproduced by permission of The Keeper of Public
Records and the UK Hydrographic Office
(www.GOV.uk/UKHO)

ISBN: 978-0-9933540-4-5

Printed in Slovenia for Latitude Press Ltd.

Rockfish – award-winning seafood restaurants
by the coast and seafood delivery to your home.
@theRockfishUK

Publisher
Jon Croft

Commissioning Editor
Meg Boas

Art Direction & Design
Marie O'Shepherd

Rockfish Project Manager
Laura Cowan

Food Photography
Chris Terry

Location Photography
Ed Ovenden

Editor
Norma Macmillan

Home Economy
Elaine Byfield

Proofreading
Margaret Haynes

Indexing
Zoe Ross

For 'Mr Blue Sky'
Wherever you are.

CONTENTS

My family and I have many wonderful memories of dining and enjoying time at Mitch's original Rockfish restaurant in Dartmouth, and I was so excited when he told me he was opening another one because it meant having another great place to go!

The concept makes complete sense: a real, down-to-earth seafood restaurant, specialising not only in amazing fish and chips, but making sure the seafood is 'happy' seafood. Mitch's ethos is that of keeping to species that are sustainable, showcasing the fish we should be eating and encouraging us to try something different, and then cooking that fish with the utmost respect.

A series of Rockfish restaurants have popped up around the south west coast in the past few years and as a family we have been lucky enough to dine in most of them. Each time we've walked in, we've received the warmest of welcomes, just as all their customers do, and been impressed by the knowledge of the front of house staff. Of course, it goes without saying that the food is always as we'd expect: generous, well cooked and, most of all, incredibly delicious!

With the publication of this amazing book, we can all now recreate those dishes at home using Mitch's easy to follow recipes. All the favourites from our family trips to Rockfish are in these pages, along with a few that will no doubt appear on Rockfish menus soon, from the traditional to the slightly more exotic, the simple to the more challenging. It's a really comprehensive collection which means that when we can't get to the restaurants, we can have a go at home – brilliant!

Adding to the recipes, Mitch has included snippets and stories together with superb photos of our beautiful coast, as well as showing how the finished dishes should look and making your mouth water. The introductions to the dishes encourage you to 'have a go', so what are you waiting for?

Mitch and the gang at Rockfish should be so proud of what they have created with this book: it's a welcome addition to my collection and it should be to yours, too.

Here's wishing you fun cooking and happy eating!

Nathan Outlaw,
Chef and restaurateur

INTRODUCTION

I have lived on the coast and enjoyed seafood for pretty much all of my life. I love the ever-changing experience of coastal and island life. No two days are the same. Clouds and wind change as weather fronts come and go, bringing big surf or beautiful calms, each welcome in their own way. The sunshine and light changes everything too; Caribbean-like seas one day and the next the very same view is a rolling grey sea crashing on the beach. To feel the warmth of the early sun as it rises in mid-June, or to marvel at the evening canvas as the setting sun paints its own picture on the sky and clouds, is, for me, one of the best things about living on the coast. I'm sure some will argue that there are even better places to live, but I won't be trying to find them; for me the British coastline is the finest in the world.

The same goes for our seafood. When I opened my first fishmonger in 1996 I was amazed at what turned up at my door every day. The variety and freshness of the produce was just marvellous, and I was filled with an energy that made me want to share that enthusiasm day after day, just as I am now.

For me, there is no doubt that British seafood is the finest in the world. When I sit and think about all the fishing ports I've visited in Britain and all the boats I've seen, it is the small fleets that I imagine. Small boats, big boats, interesting characters of all ages: this is our fishing industry. It's not on an industrial scale, but it's generations of local men and women harvesting the seas in a sustainable way as they always have. For me this is part of the magic and why our seafood is the best in the world.

The first Rockfish restaurant opened in Dartmouth in 2010, serving local fried fish for which it won a number of awards. Over the next few years, it developed into more of a seafood restaurant as we added a variety of species and new dishes, and harnessed the energy and enthusiasm of other people who joined Rockfish and embraced our mission to cook great seafood by the sea. This part of the experience is important to me; it might just be in the mind, but I believe seafood tastes better with a view of the sea, or after a walk on the beach. Try it: you'll know what I mean.

When it comes to fish cookery, freshness is everything and after that, it's simplicity. These rules have never changed for me and they still stand firm today. We apply this approach in every one of our restaurants. Our spiritual home is Brixham where we have a restaurant and fishmonger. Our boat, The Rockfisher, fishes out of Brixham harbour, and every day we buy fish at the world famous Brixham fish auction, direct from the boats. Our fishmongers are preparing it as soon as it leaves the market and by lunchtime it's in our restaurants, where our chefs, who love seafood as much as I do, cook it perfectly in our simple Rockfish style.

I've wanted to write this book for some years. Not all of the dishes are served in our restaurants but I like to think of them as Rockfish seafood nonetheless. These are dishes that I cook at home for friends and family, and I've enjoyed having no boundary or style to stick too. There's grilled fish, curries, Asian salads and more humble suppers. Each dish is easy to achieve in any kitchen and I hope you have fun cooking and sharing them.

Most of all, I hope you find the same love I have for our native seafood. It's the best in the world and caught by unique group of people and families who know our coastlines and seas better than anyone else.

Happy cooking!

ROCKFISH PLAYLIST

For a taste of our music at Rockfish, follow this code and have a listen. It's great to cook along to or take to the beach.

ROCKFISH LIFE

Apart from a love of seafood, it's also a love of the coast that binds everyone together at Rockfish. More than ever, we are cold water swimming, surfing and paddle boarding, simple activities that help us to experience the power of the 'blue gym'; it's the other side to the hard work everyone puts in every day to make sure our restaurants are the places we want them to be.

We try to find our restoration by the sea, a place where the passage of time seems to slow, with nature at its most awesome, and there is always a feeling of freedom and escape. I dream about getting on the ocean conveyor and letting the winds and tides take me round the world.

Everyone's day and coastal experience is unique; the view of sunrise and sunset is different in each port, town or estuary. At Rockfish, we like to share these experiences, commenting on each other's days as a reminder of the happiness we find here by the coast.

This page is a few of the snapshots of the British coast at its best, all taken by Rockfish staff on their days off or on a break, and then shared with their work friends. It's a lovely thing to see this every day, knowing that some of us are out there taking it all in.

The coast belongs to everyone and we love to see the steady flow of visitors throughout the year who come for their own enjoyment, peace and restoration. Our job is to be part of that experience, and who doesn't see the ocean and think of eating fresh seafood?

Rockfish
Rockfish.....?
?
Rockfish ?...
where would people like to eat seafood?
EDDYSTONE ROCKS
Dodman Pt.
The Bellows
The Bizzies
Saint Anthony
The Wriggiers
The Manacles
Manacle Pt.
Truro
5°00'W
50°00'N
49°56'2N
4°18'2W
3°45'W 2005 (9°E)

SUMMER

OYSTERS
natural & dressed

Oysters fascinate me. There is a ceremony to eating them, and their briny, fresh ozone flavour can vary from oyster to oyster just as bottles of the same wine can vary. The flavour of an oyster reflects the environment it is grown in. The UK has a number of fabulous producers. We like the oysters from Portland, from our friend Nigel Bloxham at his fabulous Crab House Café in Weymouth, Brownsea in Poole and Carlingford Lough in Northern Ireland.

Oysters vary throughout the year as they go through their breeding cycle. When they spawn they are milky and plump – I have to confess that this isn't my favourite oyster but it is for many. I like small oysters from when they are not spawning. The flavour is more briny then.

The oysters we use are rock oysters. They are farmed as opposed to being fished in the wild. When I say farmed I mean just contained – they aren't going anywhere! They are grown on racks that filter the sea water as the tide goes in and out, which forms the characteristic flavour of the oysters' environment. The French are masters at growing oysters. On some parts of the French coast they use a process called 'affinage', where the oysters start life at sea but go through a ripening finish where they gain their final flavour. This flavour varies, depending on the quality of the water they are finished in or how many oysters there are per square metre. It's quite a thing and the oysters are utterly superb. I could sit for hours with a plate of small ones, a few different dressings and a bottle of wine.

To open, or shuck, an oyster you will need an oyster knife, which has a sort of potted blade. Hold the oyster in a cloth and insert the knife into the hinge at the pointed end. You may need to wiggle the knife and push quite hard, but the oyster will pop open. Remove the top flat shell and the oyster is ready to serve 'on the half shell'.

Over the next few pages are a few dressings that work really well on freshly shucked oysters. Although I'm not a fan of cooked oysters I like this grilled Parmesan and pancetta recipe.

JALAPEÑO & LIME
Simply finely chop 2 fresh jalapeño chillies. Mix with lime juice, a dash of fish sauce and some finely chopped coriander, and spoon over each oyster.

CHILLI & GINGER
Grate some fresh ginger into 4 tablespoons rice vinegar and add 1 teaspoon sugar. Stir in finely chopped fiery red chilli to taste and spoon over the oysters.

KIMCHI DRESSING

Kimchi is a fermented vegetable mix from Korea. It's pretty delicious and works well with shellfish. Simply put a few tablespoons of kimchi in a blender with a dash of toasted sesame oil, a splash of rice vinegar and a pinch of sugar. Blitz, then dress the oysters.

PONZU & CUCUMBER

You can buy ready-made ponzu sauce or make your own (see Tempura Prawns on page 82). Simply remove the seeds from a cucumber before grating the flesh. Squeeze out excess moisture. Chill for 30 minutes, then spoon over the oysters and dress with ponzu sauce.

PARMESAN & PANCETTA

Very finely chop some pancetta and fry until crisp. Mix with a few tablespoons of double cream and a good grating of Parmesan. Finish with Worcestershire sauce to taste, then spoon on to the oysters. Scrunch up some foil and place it on a baking tray. Nestle the oysters in the foil to stop them spilling, then grill until bubbling and golden.

PRAWN & CRAB SOM TAM SALAD

Any Asian seafood recipe will be delicious. There is always an explosion of flavour in Thai salads and Malaysian and Singaporean curries. Every recipe seems to capture the whole spectrum of flavours – hot, sweet, sour, fragrant and fresh in every mouthful. One of my favourite dishes, which I enjoy almost every day on our family holidays to Thailand, is this simple salad that is served everywhere on the islands. Green papaya is the main ingredient. You can find it in Asian stores although I have made the salad successfully using courgette and cucumber cut into strips.

This is a dish I like to take to the beach. I just dress it and add the crab at the last minute, then sit with my feet in the water and with a cold beer in hand. I could be anywhere in the world.

In Thailand they have a small tool like a potato peeler that is very useful for making this salad. You just run it down the vegetables to create long strips, which are what make the salad's texture so good.

SERVES 4

2 large carrots, peeled
1 green papaya, peeled
a 15cm length of cucumber
1 red onion, sliced lengthways (root to top)
16 peeled cooked king prawns – if buying raw, poach gently in salted water
150g fresh hand-picked white crab meat
6 cherry tomatoes, quartered
a handful of mint leaves
a handful of coriander leaves

For the dressing
4–6 small garlic cloves, peeled
2 small red chillies – add more if you want it hot
1 tablespoon palm sugar
juice of 1 lime
6 tablespoons fish sauce

If you have the Thai tool, run it down the sides of each vegetable – carrots, papaya and cucumber – to create long strips. Alternatively, slice the vegetables, then cut into thin matchsticks. Place in a mixing bowl. Add the red onion.

Make the dressing by bruising the garlic with the chillies and palm sugar in a pestle and mortar. Add the lime juice and then the fish sauce and pound to mix. The dressing should be hot, sweet and salty. Pour over the vegetables and toss to dress them, then add the prawns, half the crab and the tomatoes, and toss through. Add the mint and coriander and toss in.

Serve on a big platter sprinkled with the rest of the crab.

CAESAR SALAD
with pickled sardines

Traditionally Cæsar salad is made with salted anchovies – not the white pickled ones you often see draping this classic salad. But for this dish I break my own rules, because pickled sardines are just delicious. You can buy them in Spanish delicatessens – try my friends at mevalco.com who will send their marinated sardines to you. They sell some fabulous products. If you want to pickle your own sardine fillets, see below.

We cheat on the dressing recipe and use our anchovy mayonnaise as a base for it. This was a chance discovery that changed the way we do things and I now prefer this recipe.

SERVES 2

4 tablespoons anchovy
   mayonnaise (see page 130)
a dash of Worcestershire sauce
2 garlic cloves, crushed
2 heads of romaine lettuce,
   outer leaves removed
6 pickled/marinated sardine
   fillets, drained
Parmesan for grating over
   the top

Put the mayonnaise into a large bowl. Add the Worcestershire sauce and garlic and mix it all together.

Separate the lettuce leaves, add to the bowl and gently massage in the dressing to ensure it coats each leaf. Lift them on to plates and weave the sardine fillets into the leaves. Finish with a good grating of Parmesan.

TO PICKLE SARDINES
Buy them fresh from the fishmonger and ask him to fillet them (or do this yourself). Combine 70ml white wine vinegar, 30g sugar, 30ml water and 5g salt in a pan and bring to the boil, then cool. Once cold, add a few coriander seeds. Pour over the sardine fillets and leave to pickle for 2–3 hours or overnight if you like a strong pickle.

RAW FISH – A FLAVOUR BOMB

Eating raw fish might seem a little odd to some people and for that reason it has only made a brief appearance on menus at Rockfish. But it is something we all love and I wanted to share a few of our favourite ways of preparing it. There is something really delicious about the texture of raw fish that has been 'cooked' in citrus juice. It's a simple process and each one of these dishes is a flavour bomb in the mouth. Just pop to your fishmonger and buy the freshest fish you can. Don't leave it to sit in your fridge for days. Buy it fresh and eat it fresh.

SEA BASS, FENNEL, LIME & ORANGE

If you have whole sea bass that have been filleted this is a good way to use the tails, which are less meaty than the thicker parts, and perfect to make a little plate of ceviche. Sea bass can come at a price and if it's not available then look out for mackerel, bream, grey mullet or even small lemon sole fillets. All work well prepared this way. The trick with this kind of dish is to get the textures right – thin crisp vegetables are what's called for. Think about getting everything in proportion to give it balance.

SERVES 4 AS A STARTER

280g skinless sea bass fillet
a pinch of fine salt
juice of 1 lime
juice of ½ orange
1 small fennel bulb, outer
    leaves removed
½ orange, cut into segments
½ red onion, finely sliced
a small handful of shredded
    coriander

To finish
olive oil
a pinch of smoked chilli flakes
    – Urfa chillies (optional)

Cut the fish into 1.5cm cubes. Sprinkle with salt and leave for a few minutes, then pour over the lime and orange juices and place in the fridge. Leave to 'cook' for up to 10 minutes.

Meanwhile, thinly slice the fennel on a mandoline and drop into a bowl of iced water to keep it crisp.

Add the drained fennel and remaining ingredients to the fish and toss together. Divide among serving plates. Add a drizzle of olive oil and a sprinkle of smoked chilli flakes, if using.

SEA BREAM TARTARE

This is one of my favourite ways to prepare raw fish. I like the contrast between delicate seafood, crunch and pickle. It makes a wonderful starter. If you want to make it look more like a restaurant dish you can lightly press it into a ring. The American mustard is much milder than English or French but has a great flavour that doesn't overpower the fish.

SERVES 4

3 tablespoons olive oil
juice of ½ lemon
¼ teaspoon French's American-style mustard
a pinch of white pepper
1 sea bream, weighing about 450g, filleted and skin removed, then cut into 1.5cm cubes
1 tablespoon salted capers, rinsed and chopped

1 large shallot, finely chopped
6 green olives, finely chopped
1 tablespoon finely chopped tarragon
1 tablespoon finely chopped chives
1 green chilli, deseeded and finely chopped
1 large dill pickle, finely chopped
salt

Put the olive oil, lemon juice and mustard into a bowl and whisk together. Season to your taste and to balance the flavours – it's important to get it right as this will be the background flavour of the dish. When you're happy, add everything else and gently stir together, then serve.

CEVICHE OF SALMON, DILL & CELERY

Salmon is particularly good raw and in dishes like this it takes on other flavours really well. With the crunch of the celery, fresh limes and red onion, this is a classic ceviche.

SERVES 4 AS A STARTER

280g skinless salmon fillet – I like the fatty belly part but if that's not for you then a slice from the middle or tail will work well too
a good pinch of fine salt
juice of 2 limes

1 celery stick, strings peeled and finely sliced
a small handful of chopped dill
6 mint leaves, roughly chopped
¼ red onion, finely sliced
2 tablespoons olive oil
½ teaspoon red peppercorns

Cut the fish into rough chunks about 1.5cm. Sprinkle with salt and then with lime juice. Leave in the fridge for up to 10 minutes to allow the fish to 'cook'.

Add the remaining ingredients, except the oil and peppercorns, and toss together. Lift the mixture on to plates and pour over the juices. Drizzle over the olive oil, then crush the peppercorns over the top and serve.

THE MACKEREL SCHWARMA

I love the flavours of a good kebab so here they are with one of my favourite fish. This really is a flavour explosion. There's lots going on, from the smokiness of the mackerel to the garlic yoghurt, fresh herbs and a crunchy salad. Well worth making.

SERVES 2

1 mackerel, filleted and skinned
1 heaped tablespoon plain flour
a pinch of ground cloves
a pinch of ground cardamom
a pinch of ground cinnamon
a pinch of white pepper
olive oil for frying

For the smoked mackerel 'hummus'

1 smoked mackerel fillet, skinned
80g drained canned chickpeas, rinsed
1 tablespoon tahini
2 tablespoons mayonnaise (see recipe on page 131)
zest of ½ lemon

For the garlic yoghurt

1 garlic clove, crushed
2 tablespoons plain yoghurt

To assemble

75g white cabbage, finely sliced
juice of 1 lemon
2 flour tortillas
1 tomato, chopped
½ small red onion, finely sliced (root to top)
a small bunch of dill, chopped
za'atar – a Lebanese spice sold in most supermarkets
1 fresh green chilli, finely sliced
a pinch of chilli flakes
2 tablespoons pomegranate seeds
salt

To make the 'hummus', combine the mackerel, chickpeas and tahini in a food processor and blitz to a smooth paste. Transfer to a bowl and fold in the mayonnaise and lemon zest. Set aside until ready to serve.

Mix the garlic with the yoghurt and a good pinch of salt. Dress the cabbage with lemon juice.

Remove any pinbones from the mackerel fillets. Mix the flour with the cloves, cardamom, cinnamon and pepper. Dip the mackerel fillets in this to coat both sides, then fry in a little olive oil, skinned side down, for about 2 minutes or until crisp. Turn on to the other side and finish cooking for about 1 minute. Leave in the pan, off the heat.

Warm the tortillas, then lay them out and spread the 'hummus' over them. Scatter over the cabbage, then the tomato and onion followed by plenty of dill. Lay a mackerel fillet on each. Add a tablespoon of garlic yoghurt, then sprinkle liberally with za'atar, fresh chilli, chilli flakes and pomegranate seeds. Fold the bottom in and wrap it all up.

PLAICE MILANESE
with warm tartare sauce _____

This is a very nice way to prepare plaice, which has a particular texture and flavour. It's okay grilled and nice tranches are good roasted on the bone, but I don't think anything can beat it cooked in breadcrumbs. This somehow brings out the best in this fish. As it is so delicate, the acidity and texture of a good chunky tartare sauce makes a perfect foil.

Plaice start to become good around May and they get fatter and juicier as the year goes on, well into August. If you can get a fillet from a kilo-plus-sized fish you can cut it into 4 portions. I think these are the best.

SERVES 2

2 handfuls of plain flour
2 eggs, beaten
2 handfuls of panko
    breadcrumbs
2 portions of plaice fillet,
    weighing about 180g each,
    skinned (unless you like to
    eat the skin)
vegetable oil for frying
6 tablespoons Rockfish tartare
    (see page 130)
a small handful of chopped
    parsley (optional)
lemon wedges to serve

Put the flour, eggs and breadcrumbs on separate plates. Using one hand dip the fish in the flour, then the eggs and then the breadcrumbs, making sure you get a nice even coating. Repeat with the other fish portion.

Put about 1cm of vegetable oil in a pan and heat to about 160°C. (If you don't have a thermometer, heat the oil until a small piece of bread dropped in quickly fizzles and crisps.) Lay the fish in the hot oil and fry for 2–3 minutes on each side or until crisp and golden, then drain on kitchen paper.

Warm the tartare sauce in a pan, then divide between 2 plates and spread out over the plate. Place the fish on top, sprinkle with parsley, if using, and serve with lemon wedges.

LOBSTER & CRAB

I don't think there is anything better to eat than a south coast crab. My favourite meal is a freshly boiled crab, picked whilst warm and eaten with fresh bread and mayonnaise – utterly perfect.

Crabs and lobsters are caught from rocky coastlines all around the UK, and in the main are sent off to China and Europe. I can understand that tackling crabs and lobster might prove challenging to some people; however, it looks harder than it is and, once mastered, it is a skill for life and opens up a whole new world of wonderful dishes and experiences.

STEAMED LOBSTER
with herb butter & fries

Just as you cannot beat the simplicity of crab and mayonnaise, I feel it's the same with lobster and melted butter, or drawn butter as the Americans call it. To enjoy it at its best, the lobster needs to be still warm and the butter just melted – you don't want cold lobster going into hot butter. If you are finding it hard to set up a steamer just boil the lobster in plenty of salted water for 12 minutes and leave it to drain, then split it while it's still warm.

SERVES 2

2 x 500g live lobsters
oven-cook fries to serve
60g salted butter
½ tablespoon chopped
    tarragon
½ tablespoon chopped parsley
a squeeze of lemon juice
a pinch of white pepper

Chill the lobsters well. Put each lobster in turn on a chopping board, lay a tea towel over the tail and hold the tail down. Insert a large cook's knife down through the cross on the back of the lobster's head, which will kill it instantly. Set up a steamer and bring the water to a rolling boil. Steam the lobsters for 15–20 minutes, then remove and cool a bit.

Meanwhile, cook the fries as indicated on the packet. Melt the butter gently, then add the herbs, lemon juice and pepper. Keep warm.

Split the lobsters in half and crack the claws. Serve with the herb butter and fries. Pull the meat from the shell, dip into the butter and enjoy with a crisp fry.

CRAB CAKES

This is an American classic, incredibly simple and delicious, well worth making for a starter or light lunch. Be flexible with flavours: if you like chilli, make the crab cakes hot, or add a little curry powder to give them a spicy kick. Just follow the basic recipe and make them your own. We made these at Rockfish for a short while with spider crab, which were wonderfully delicious.

MAKES 8

250g fresh hand-picked white crabmeat
45g fresh breadcrumbs
a pinch of ground mace
a pinch of white pepper
a pinch of grated nutmeg
a pinch of English mustard powder or 1 teaspoon English mustard

a small handful of chopped parsley
1 egg, beaten
about 3 tablespoons plain flour for coating
2–3 tablespoons vegetable oil for frying
salt

Simply mix everything together, with the exception of the flour and oil, and season with salt. Shape into 8 patties about 2.5cm thick. Chill for 15 minutes to firm them up.

Dust in flour to coat. Heat the oil in a frying pan and fry the crab cakes for 5–6 minutes or until both sides are lightly browned and crisp and they are warmed through.

OUR CRAB ROLL

This is the way we make our crab roll at Rockfish. First, the right bread makes all the difference: you need a soft white roll, either a bun or finger roll. Soft and squidgy with no real crust, just a light golden colour and a slight chew to it. We played around with all sorts of delicious flavour combinations but, in the end, it's all about the crab. It only needs a little crunch and some light acidity, which we found in the pickles that we include and from the Little Gem.

SERVES 1

½ Little Gem lettuce – the sweet inner leaves are best
a 5cm piece of cucumber, peeled, cored and finely chopped
1 dill pickle, finely chopped
2 tablespoons mayonnaise – your favourite brand
or make your own (see recipe on page 131)
1 soft white roll
butter
fresh hand-picked white crabmeat – enough to fill your roll
white pepper

Finely shred the lettuce and mix with the cucumber, dill pickle and mayonnaise. Season with white pepper.

Split open the roll, butter and then gently toast in a deep frying pan until golden brown. Spread the lettuce mix on the bottom half of the roll, then top with as much crab meat as you can comfortably fit in!

DRESSED CRAB
& mayonnaise

Perhaps the simplest and yet most delicious way to eat a fresh crab. Cooking a crab is not hard; it just takes a little time. It's well worth mastering for all the trips to the seaside when you can use this skill to crack one open while you sit on a beach, feet in the surf, cold beer at hand.

SERVES 2

1 crab, weighing about 1kg – cock crabs have tiger claws and more white meat, while hen crabs have smaller claws and less white meat but more delicious brown meat – place in the freezer for 4 hours before cooking to knock it out
mayonnaise – your favourite brand or make your own (see recipe on page 131)
chopped parsley
a few slices of cucumber
a few slices of lemon
bread and butter to serve
salt

Bring a big pan of water to the boil with a handful of salt in it and drop the crab straight into the water. Bring back to the boil and cook for about 15 minutes. Remove the crab and stand on its nose to drain and cool. Fish out legs that may have been ejected by the crab during cooking.

When the crab has cooled turn it on to its back and open it up: put your thumbs under the back legs and push up until the crab pops apart (this can be difficult but it will open). Keep the top shell for serving (clean and dry it) as well as the brown meat but drain off any water. Discard the dead man's fingers – the small feathery things on the body (you may also find some in the top shell if they have become detached during opening).

Pull off the claws and crack them with a heavy object like a rolling pin, using just enough force to break the shell. Then simply pick out the meat with the handle of a fork or a skewer, trying to get it out in as big chunks as you can. Pull off the legs and do the same. Cut the body into 6 by first cutting it in half, top to bottom, then slicing in between the legs so each leg has a clump of body at the end of it. Pick out every last bit of meat you can find. I like to do this with my fingers.

Scrape the dark meat from the top shell and mix it together with the mayo and parsley until it's nice and smooth. You may have some 'soft shell', which looks like shell but is soft. Mash this in – it is wonderful. If there are any red roes, which are the eggs in a hen crab, mash this in too. Present the crab as in the picture, with the cucumber and lemon. Serve with bread and butter and a little extra mayo on the side.

SINGAPORE CHILLI CRAB

If you have ever visited Singapore you will have experienced the famous, very delicious chilli crab. It is the national dish. Easy to make, it is a firm favourite in the Tonks household, and chilli crab night is an occasion that brings the family together. Instructions for cooking a fresh crab are in the recipe for Dressed Crab on page 39.

SERVES 2

1 cooked crab, weighing about 1kg – hen or cock crab is fine as they both work well; size is up to you and your appetite
4 tablespoons cornflour
vegetable oil for deep-frying

For the paste
8 fresh red chillies, roughly chopped
75g peeled fresh ginger, roughly chopped
4 garlic cloves, peeled
1 tablespoon shrimp paste – you can buy this in Asian stores; it's smelly but adds an incredible flavour to the dish
vegetable oil for frying

For the sauce
2 tablespoons palm sugar or soft brown sugar
4 tablespoons tomato ketchup
2 tablespoons sriracha chilli sauce
1 tablespoon soy sauce
200ml chicken stock – I use Knorr powder
2 eggs, beaten

To garnish
2 spring onions, finely sliced
a handful of chopped coriander

Open the crab: place it on its back, put your thumbs under the back legs and push up until the crab pops apart (this can be difficult but it will open). Keep the top shell (clean and dry it) and the brown meat but drain off any water and discard the dead man's fingers – the small feathery things on the body (you may also find some in the top shell) – and any membrane. Pull off the claws, cut them in half and give the pieces a good crack so the sauce will be able to get into the meat. Cut the body into 6 by first cutting it in half, top to bottom, then slicing in between the legs so each leg has a clump of body at the end of it.

Put the pieces of crab body and claws in a bowl. Sprinkle over the cornflour and toss, making sure everything is completely coated. This will give the crab a nice stickiness when it's cooked. Heat the oil in a deep pan to about 160°C. (If you don't have a thermometer or deep-fat fryer, heat the oil in a deep pan – it is hot enough to fry the crab when a small piece of bread dropped in quickly fizzles and crisps.)

Working in batches, deep-fry all the pieces of crab for about 3 minutes, then drain on kitchen paper.

To make the paste, blitz the chillies, ginger, garlic and shrimp paste together in a food processor. Get your wok or large frying pan nice and hot, then add a little oil and fry the paste for a few minutes. Add the sugar followed by the ketchup, sriracha and soy. Stir together, then add the stock and mix well.

Add the pieces of crab and the brown crab meat and cook for 5–6 minutes.

Remove the crab and place on your serving dish or in the crab shell, if using for decoration. Turn up the heat under the wok and stir the beaten eggs into the sauce. As soon as you start to see strands of white appear, remove from the heat and pour the sauce over the crab. Garnish with spring onions and coriander and serve.

FRESH CRAB
with tzatziki & tomato

You will be surprised at how good this tastes. It's an easy assembly and makes a delicious starter or summer lunch.

SERVES 2

2 beef tomatoes
100g fresh hand-picked
   white crabmeat

For the tzatziki
½ cucumber, peeled
150ml full-fat Greek yoghurt
1 garlic clove, crushed
a squeeze of lemon juice
a small handful of chopped dill
1 teaspoon dried mint, or
   1 tablespoon chopped
   fresh mint
salt

Grate the cucumber to the seeded core; discard this core. Squeeze the grated cucumber in a muslin cloth or your hands to remove any excess moisture. Place in a bowl and add the rest of the tzatziki ingredients. Mix everything together, then let it sit in the fridge for an hour or so for the flavours to develop.

Cut the tomatoes in half and scoop out the seeds. Place 2 halves on each plate and season the insides with salt. Half fill with tzatziki, then heap on the crab.

That's it!

CRAB HUMMUS

This is a good combination. Make your own hummus so you can flavour it to your taste. You want it nice and smooth with a good balance of lemon and tahini and not too much garlic. I don't normally have much use for brown crabmeat from hen crabs when there's lots of roe; although it is really tasty, it can be dry. However, it is the best dark meat to use for this dish. Buy the best white crabmeat you can. Hand-picked is best.

SERVES 2

200g drained chickpeas, rinsed – I use the Spanish ones in jars but canned is fine too
juice of 1 lemon
1 garlic clove, peeled
a pinch of salt
1 teaspoon tahini
4 tablespoons olive oil
75g fresh brown crabmeat

150g fresh hand-picked white crabmeat
1 teaspoon finely chopped dill
1 tomato, cored and finely chopped
½ avocado, peeled and finely chopped
2 spring onions, green part finely sliced

Put the chickpeas in a food processor with half of the lemon juice, the garlic clove, salt and tahini. Blitz, then add the olive oil and blitz again until smooth. Fold in the brown crabmeat.

Toss the white crab meat with the dill, tomato, avocado and remaining lemon juice. To serve, spread the brown crab tahini mix in a bowl and top with the white crabmeat mix and the sliced spring onions.

CRAB SLAW

With chips, with fish, on its own, in a bun, as a salad, this is just great. The trick is not to add too much mayo or you'll drown out the sweet crab. Slice your vegetables as thinly as possible – a mandoline is good for this.

In this version of the recipe I've used just the white meat but if you want to add a bit more crab flavour just stir a tablespoon of brown meat through the mayo.

SERVES 4–6

2 large carrots, peeled
2 large-bulbed spring onions
150g white cabbage
½–1 fennel bulb (depending on size)
a 15cm length of cucumber
1 celery stick, sliced on an angle

6 tablespoons lemon mayo (see page 131)
200g fresh hand-picked white crabmeat
a small amount of chopped dill (optional)
salt and white pepper

Shred all the vegetables into fine matchsticks or strips. Bind with the mayonnaise and season with salt and pepper. Fold in the crab and dill, if using, and serve.

ROCKFISH ON THE WATER

Away from seafood our passion for sailing and the seas run as deep as the waters that surround us at Rockfish; from engaging in the stewardship of our oceans to playing a small part in helping local youngsters navigate their sailing aspirations.

CRISP-FRIED SOFT-SHELL CRAB ROLL
with Korean chilli slaw

The gochujang paste used in flavouring this dish is a salted fermented paste used in Korean cooking. It's not hot but adds a wonderful flavour to seafood. You can get it in any Asian store but as it is becoming increasingly popular, it can be found in some supermarkets. If you can't find it use sriracha, which is more widely available, and add a squeeze of lime juice.

SERVES 2

2 soft white bridge or
   brioche rolls
2 soft-shell crabs
a handful of rice flour
vegetable oil for deep-frying

For the slaw
a squeeze of lime juice
1 teaspoon caster sugar
1 garlic clove, grated
a 2.5cm piece of fresh ginger,
   peeled and grated
4 tablespoons mayonnaise
   – your favourite brand or
   make your own (see recipe
   on page 131)
1 tablespoon gochujang paste
a dash of fish sauce
a dash of toasted sesame oil
a handful of finely shredded
   Chinese leaf cabbage
2 spring onions, finely chopped
1 tablespoon chopped mint
1 large carrot, peeled and cut
   into shreds on a mandoline

Split the rolls open and lightly toast the insides.

Mix the lime juice with the sugar, then add the garlic and ginger. Stir in the mayo and gochujang and season with the fish sauce and sesame oil. Toss the cabbage, spring onions, mint and carrot in the sauce. Spoon on to the base of the rolls.

Heat the oil to 170°C. (If you don't have a thermometer or deep-fat fryer, heat the oil in a deep pan – it is hot enough to fry the crab when a small piece of bread dropped in quickly fizzles and crisps.)

Dip the crabs in water and then in the rice flour.

Deep-fry the crab in the hot oil for 5–7 minutes or until crisp. Drain well on kitchen paper, then sit on top of the slaw. Serve the rolls open or closed.

THERMIDOR BUTTERED CRAB
on toast

This is a nice buttery mix. You make the butter first, then chill it in the fridge to firm it up. The butter is really good with all grilled seafood but on toast with crab it makes a wonderful snack. The recipe makes more butter than you need so you will have some to store in the fridge or freezer to top plain grilled seafood.

SERVES 2

2 slices bread for toasting
150g fresh hand-picked
   white crabmeat

For the butter
1 shallot, finely chopped
a splash of brandy or dry sherry
100ml white wine
1 tablespoon Dijon mustard
1 tablespoon chopped parsley
1 tablespoon chopped tarragon
150g salted butter, at room
   temperature
a splash of double cream
a pinch of cayenne pepper
4 tablespoons grated Parmesan
   plus extra for grilling
salt and freshly ground
   black pepper

First make the butter. Put the shallot, brandy or dry sherry and white wine in a pan and boil off the alcohol. Transfer the shallot to a bowl and cool a little, then add the remaining ingredients and fold together. Taste and season. Roll into a sausage in clingfilm and chill until firm, or freeze for longer storage.

Preheat the grill and toast the bread.

Melt half the butter in a pan. When it is warm, stir in the crabmeat until warmed through. Spoon on to the toast. Grate some Parmesan over the top, then grill for a few minutes until slightly golden. Serve.

CHARGRILLED MONKFISH
with lime pickle butter

Definitely try this! The butter is fabulously salty, tangy, savoury and hot, and it works well with all grilled seafood. I have to credit the recipe to Jossy Dimbleby, whose books I used when I was teaching myself to cook. It was after a chat with her son, Henry, who was telling me about an amazing chicken dish that she made with lime pickle butter rubbed under the skin, that my mind instantly turned to seafood and I made my own version. It is very, very good!

SERVES 2

1 monkfish tail, weighing
  about 800g, skin and
  membrane removed
olive oil
2 fresh green chillies,
  finely sliced
salt

For the lime pickle butter
2 tablespoons lime pickle –
  I like the East End brand but
  Pataks is good too
1 tablespoon mango chutney –
  I use a hot one but you don't
  have to
1 garlic clove, peeled
2 handfuls of coriander plus
  extra chopped to garnish
vegetable oil for frying
1 teaspoon black mustard seeds
12–15 curry leaves
125g salted butter, at room
  temperature
zest and juice of 1 lime

The monkfish is best cooked on a barbecue, but if that's not possible then use a hot ridged grill pan as a second choice, or an overhead grill or very hot oven (you will just miss the smoky charred bits). First butterfly the fish (you might want to ask your fishmonger to do this as it is a little tricky). Cut down one side along the bone but not going all the way through so the fillet is still attached at one edge. Turn the fish over and do the same on the opposite side. Remove the bone. Keep the fish in the fridge.

Put the lime pickle, mango chutney, garlic and coriander in a blender and blitz until smooth. Transfer to a bowl. Put a little oil in a small frying pan and fry the mustard seeds until they pop. Add the curry leaves and fry for a few more minutes, then add to the bowl with the blitzed lime pickle mix. Add the softened butter and lime zest and mix it all together well. Shape into a roll wrapped in clingfilm and chill to set.

Rub the fish with olive oil and a little salt, then either barbecue, chargrill, grill or roast in your oven set to maximum for 15 minutes or until cooked. Transfer the fish to a serving plate. Place slices of the lime pickle butter on the fish, allowing the butter to melt over the fish. Finish with a squeeze of lime juice and a sprinkle of coriander and green chilli.

FRIED SPRATS
with garlic & parsley

In August we start to see the first landing of sprats. These small fish are a British delicacy. I remember eating loads as a kid, holding the head and tail and nibbling off each fillet, to be left with an almost cartoon-like fish frame. I wish I could share some magic recipe for these little fish but as ever simplicity is the magic.

SERVES 2

2 garlic cloves, peeled
a handful of flat-leaf parsley
vegetable oil for shallow frying
500g sprats – they don't need any prep, you can eat the lot; but see below if you're squeamish
a handful of plain flour
sea salt

Chop the garlic and parsley together until they are both fine.

Place about 1cm of oil in a frying pan and heat. Dip the sprats in flour to coat, then fry in the hot oil for about 2 minutes or until golden and crisp on both sides, turning them once. Divide the fish between 2 plates, season with salt and scatter the garlic and parsley mix over them.

PREPARING SPRATS
If you don't want to eat the whole sprats, remove the heads and guts and rinse, then pat the fish dry with kitchen paper before dipping in flour.

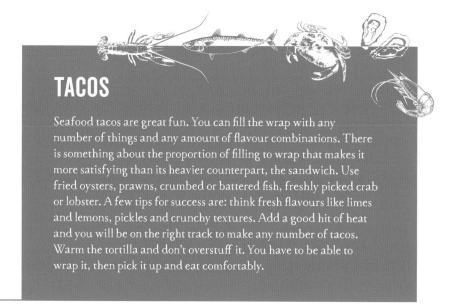

TACOS

Seafood tacos are great fun. You can fill the wrap with any number of things and any amount of flavour combinations. There is something about the proportion of filling to wrap that makes it more satisfying than its heavier counterpart, the sandwich. Use fried oysters, prawns, crumbed or battered fish, freshly picked crab or lobster. A few tips for success are: think fresh flavours like limes and lemons, pickles and crunchy textures. Add a good hit of heat and you will be on the right track to make any number of tacos. Warm the tortilla and don't overstuff it. You have to be able to wrap it, then pick it up and eat comfortably.

PRAWN & JALAPEÑO TACO

Who doesn't love sweet prawns? Add avocado, some cumin and fiery chilli, plus a squeeze of fresh lime juice and you have a simple but potent mix. Try to find Norwegian prawns that have the MSC blue tick. This is a sustainable choice and the prawns are extra good. When you find a fishmonger that sells them, ask to buy them frozen and not already thawed – once thawed they lose flavour and texture pretty quickly. The best way to thaw them is in a bowl of cold tap water, just until they start to soften when squeezed between the thumb and forefinger. If you cannot find frozen Norwegian prawns use cooked king prawns, which have a nice firm texture.

MAKES 4 TACOS

300g cooked shell-on prawns
1 avocado
½ teaspoon ground cumin
juice of 1 lime
4 flour tortillas
4 spring onions, finely sliced –
  both green and white parts
a small handful of shredded
  coriander
2 green chillies, finely sliced
  – jalapeños are best, seeds
  removed if you want less heat
salt

Peel the prawns and set aside. Cut the avocado in half and scoop out the flesh into a bowl. Roughly mash it – you want some texture, so not too smooth. Add the cumin and lime juice and season with a pinch of salt. Taste – it should be spicy, fresh and salty.

To assemble, toast the tortillas in a dry hot pan, then place on a plate and start building the tacos. Put on a spoonful of avocado first, then add a sprinkle of spring onions, coriander and chilli. Finish with a nice heap of prawns. Season with salt and serve all ready to fold and eat.

CRISP-FRIED FISH TACO
with pickles & chopped salsa verde

Gurnard, cod, pollack, monkfish, mackerel, prawns – literally any fish will work in this taco. If you don't want to deep-fry the fish, simply grill it, barbecue it or pan-fry it.

MAKES 4 TACOS

8 finger-sized pieces of skinless fish fillet
3 tablespoons plain flour
1 egg, beaten
a handful of fine dry breadcrumbs
vegetable oil for deep-frying
4 flour tortillas
a small handful of finely shredded Little Gem

4 tablespoons chopped salsa verde (see page 132)
chilli sauce or mayo (use your favourite brand or for homemade see recipe on page 131) to serve
salt and freshly ground black pepper

Dry the pieces of fish with kitchen paper. Dip the fish in flour, then egg and then breadcrumbs to coat evenly all over. Set aside ready for frying.

Heat a deep pan of oil to 170°C. (If you don't have a thermometer or deep-fat fryer, heat the oil in a deep pan – it is hot enough to fry the fish when a small piece of bread dropped in quickly fizzles and crisps.) Meanwhile, warm the tortillas under the grill or in a hot dry pan (I sometimes like to blister them on the gas ring).

Deep-fry the fish for about 4 minutes or until crisp, then season. Put each tortilla on a plate and heap on the lettuce, then the salsa verde. Place the fish on top. A blob of chilli sauce or plain mayo can work nicely on top. Wrap and enjoy.

FISH-FINGER TACO FOR ONE

Is it a taco? Is it a wrap? Is it a fish-finger sandwich? It's all of these. This is not really a recipe, more a construction job! It's something I've seen our chefs making and eating, and you can't beat it when you are in need of a quick Scooby snack.

SERVES 1

shredded iceberg lettuce
Rockfish tartare (see page 130)
1 flour tortilla
vegetable oil for frying

2 fish fingers – your favourite brand
tomato ketchup (optional)

Toss the lettuce with tartare sauce. Toast your tortilla in a dry pan.

Add a little oil to the pan and fry the fish fingers until cooked, lay them on the tortilla and top with the lettuce, then wrap it up with ketchup or not, your choice. Hey presto, a simple and delicious taco!

CUTTLEFISH

Ton after ton of cuttlefish is landed at Brixham each year and nearly all of it heads out of the country to places like Spain and Italy who have a real taste for it. It is a real shame because it is so delicious and versatile: it can be grilled, curried, braised or fried and its texture and flavour, whilst similar to squid, is better, in my opinion. In braised dishes it becomes soft and gelatinous, and in curries it adds real depth – just make your favourite fish curry and slow cook some cuttlefish in it; you will be amazed.

It's a pretty messy seafood to prepare, which may put people off, but a skilled fishmonger will do all the work if you ask them. At our restaurants we serve it instead of squid as it's so delicious and plentiful – we call it 'Brixham calamari'.

CUTTLEFISH 'AL MATTONE'
with garlic, lemon & parsley

You may wonder why I've introduced an Italian word to this dish – 'al mattone', which literally means 'under a brick'. In Italy they use this method of flattening when cooking chicken, and I've done the same here with cuttlefish. I think the Italian sounds much better than 'cooked under a brick'. You can grill the cuttlefish over fire or sear it in a red hot frying pan, placing the 'brick' on top. In the restaurants we use a commercial burger iron, which is like a small weight with a handle, to press the cuttlefish down. You can use anything with a bit of weight for a 'brick'. Just wrap it in foil first.

SERVES 2

2 garlic cloves
100ml good olive oil plus extra for brushing
a handful of chopped flat-leaf parsley
juice of ½ lemon
a pinch of dried thyme
a small handful of fine dry breadcrumbs – panko for a crisp result
2 cleaned cuttlefish
salt

Make the dressing first: grate the garlic into the olive oil, then add the parsley, lemon juice and a good pinch of salt. Set aside.

Heat your barbecue grill until the coals are white.

Mix the thyme with the breadcrumbs. Brush the cuttlefish with olive oil and season, then give it a light sprinkling of breadcrumbs on both sides. Lay it on the grill and place the weight on top. Cook for 5 minutes, then turn over, put the weight back on top and cook for a further 4 minutes.

If you are using a heavy frying pan, rub it with oil and get it hot, then cook the cuttlefish, with the weight on top, as above. You will have a nice golden colour to the cuttlefish. Serve dressed with plenty of the dressing.

CRISPY FRIED SALT-&-PEPPER CUTTLEFISH
Brixham 'calamari'

Most chefs are big fans of cuttlefish. It really is one of the most versatile and delicious of all seafoods. It's wonderful braised, when it becomes soft and giving, or cut thinly and fried until crisp (it is far better than fried calamari). If simply grilled whole it needs nothing more than a little oil and lemon to enjoy its luxurious buttery texture. I've wanted to put it on the menu for a long time but always thought the word cuttlefish would put people off. The European word sepia, which I do like, is even harder to get to grips with. So I thought 'Brixham calamari' would be a fair way to accurately describe how it actually tastes and where it comes from – we have tons of cuttlefish landed here in the port (most is sent abroad, so another great reason to eat more of it here). Definitely get your fishmonger to clean the cuttlefish – it is messy – then wash it well to remove the ink. You may still have a bit of black ink about but don't worry about it.

This is a nice easy recipe. The frying time is quick and you can easily make the dish at home.

SERVES 4 AS A STARTER

400g cleaned cuttlefish
2 good handfuls of rice flour
vegetable oil for deep-frying
2½ tablespoons salt and pepper mix (see page 133)
1 fresh red chilli, thinly sliced
2 spring onions, thinly sliced on the bias
1 lime, cut into wedges

Cut the cuttlefish into thin strips about the width of a pencil. Cut the tentacles into chunks. Put it all into a container of water. Place the rice flour in another container next to it.

Heat the oil in a deep pan to 170°C. (If you don't have a thermometer or deep-fat fryer, heat the oil in a deep pan – it is hot enough to fry the squid when a small piece of bread dropped in quickly fizzles and crisps.) In small batches take the cuttlefish from the water and dip into the flour, giving it a good massage to get a sticky but light coating on the strips of cuttlefish, then slip into the hot oil. Fry for about 2 minutes or until firm, pale and crisp. Drain on kitchen paper.

When all the cuttlefish has been fried put it into a bowl and liberally sprinkle over the salt and pepper mix. Give it a good shake about. Serve sprinkled with the sliced chilli and spring onions, and with lime wedges.

THE CUTTLEFISH & SHRIMP BURGER

I love the fish balls you get in Thai soups, and the fried cuttlefish cake in dim sum restaurants. Both have a pleasantly firm but silky 'bite' texture that is so appealing. This comes from cuttlefish that has been blitzed in a food processor to break down the proteins. Roughly chopped king prawns give a nice contrast in texture to the smooth cuttlefish. I'm being a bit American calling this shrimp in the title, I just think it sounds more appealing in a burger recipe name.

MAKES 6

For the burgers
300g cleaned cuttlefish or
    squid, roughly chopped
150g skinless white fish fillet
    such as pollock or cod,
    roughly chopped
a bunch of spring onions,
    finely chopped
juice of 1 lime
a good dash of fish sauce
1 teaspoon freshly
    grated ginger
200g peeled raw king prawns,
    roughly chopped
a small handful of coriander
light olive or vegetable oil
    for frying
salt and white pepper

To serve
4 tablespoons mayonnaise
    – your favourite brand or
    make your own (see recipe
    on page 131)
1 tablespoon sriracha chilli
    sauce, or to taste (optional)
6 soft rolls or burger buns
lettuce leaves
6 slices of beef tomato
6 slices of red onion
spring onions, finely sliced
a handful of chopped coriander
lime juice

Put the cuttlefish, white fish, spring onions, lime juice, fish sauce and ginger into a food processor and pulse until a thick paste is formed. Remove to a bowl. Mix in the chopped prawns and coriander, season then chill for an hour to firm up.

Meanwhile, mix the mayonnaise with sriracha to your taste (add more if you want it hotter) or just use plain mayo, perhaps with a dash of lime if heat isn't your thing.

Shape the fish mixture into burgers, thinner rather than thicker. Gently fry in an oiled pan for 6–7 minutes or until the burgers are firm and caramelised on both sides.

Slice the buns open and lightly toast them, then spread the cut side of the bottom half with the sriracha mayo. Lay the lettuce on top, then the tomato and onion, and then the burger. Sprinkle with the spring onions and coriander, finish with a squeeze of lime and a bit more mayo and top it with the lid.

A SHELLFISH SUPPER
family style _____

This is a favourite meal in our home and how we celebrate Christmas Eve. I have always enjoyed the French way of eating fruits de mer – there is nothing like being presented with a grand stack of shellfish. Our shellfish suppers are inspired by this but we do things less formally.

Our suppers include
crab – always
lobster – in the summer
langoustines – when we can
oysters – always
Norwegian fjord
    prawns – always
crevettes – always
steamed mussels – in winter
    (see Mussels Steamed with
    Wine, Bay, Chilli and Parsley
    on page 106)
whelks – when we can
brown shrimps – when we can
scallops – always, grilled with
    garlic (just brush with butter,
    sprinkle with finely chopped
    garlic and grill on the half
    shell for 4–5 minutes)

To accompany
crusty bread
mayonnaise – your favourite
    brand or make your own
    (see recipe on page 131)
Marie Rose sauce (see
    page 130)
sauce mignonette (see
    page 133)
malt vinegar
sriracha chilli sauce
dill pickles
pickled veg (see page 136)
wedges of lemon

The recipe is simple. Cover your table in newspaper and lay up the table with plates, cutlery and glasses. Fill the table with as many varieties of shellfish as you can, plus some crusty bread, mayonnaise, sauces and pickles and lemon wedges. Then just enjoy the next few hours. When it comes to cleaning up simply wrap up all the empty shells and other debris in the newspaper.

WINTER

FRITTO MISTO

If there's a dish I often crave, it's this one. The name means 'mixed fried', and that's all it is. No batter needed, just water, flour and fresh seafood. It not really a full blown recipe as you can use whatever you like and any quantities depending on how many you're feeding, but here's how I do it.

SERVES AS MANY AS YOU WISH

selection of super fresh seafood
  – I use squid, small scallops,
  red mullet, cuttlefish,
  cockles, prawns and/or cod
rice flour, to coat
vegetable oil, for frying
a handful of finely chopped
  parsley (optional)
lemon wedges to serve

You need 2 containers, one with water and one with rice flour.

Heat the oil in a deep pan to 170°C. (If you don't have a thermometer or deep-fat fryer, heat the oil in a deep pan – it is hot enough to fry the seafood when a small piece of bread dropped in quickly fizzles and crisps.)

Add all the seafood to the container with the water, and then, a few pieces at a time, dip in the rice flour to coat and slip into the hot oil to fry until crisp (this doesn't take long, only about 2 minutes). Don't overfill the pan with batches of seafood as this will cool the oil temperature too fast. Once fried, drain on kitchen paper, sprinkle with parsley, if using, and enjoy with plenty of lemon wedges.

ROCKFISH FISH & CHIPS_____

I asked Kirk, who looks after all the Rockfish kitchens and works on recipes with me, how he makes our chips so good. He is a stickler for making sure the chips are perfect every day.

First, the potatoes. There are many varieties and after sampling we decided the Agria potato provided us with what we want to achieve from the Rockfish chip: 'Crispy as a brand new £50 note and as fluffy as a summer cloud'. The 'chip test' is a daily ritual right before service. The kitchen team checks the blanch and finishing times by tasting the chips in detail, to ensure they are the best they can be.

We don't completely peel the potatoes as we want you to enjoy some of the skin, and we don't cut them in a uniform way. Instead they go through a blade that cut them into different sizes. So in the mix you have small, thin chips that crisp perfectly alongside thicker-cut chips. Together they create a unique chip-eating experience – you look at them and can pick a fat and fluffy one, then next a small and crisp chip or a dark and crispy bit. It's a good plate of chips.

Now the fish. This is how we do it at Rockfish but then we have all the kit to get it just right without the temperature of the oil dropping, which causes the batter to go soggy. My advice would be: it's good to know what makes great fish and chips but go somewhere specialist to enjoy them.

SERVES 2

oil for deep-frying
1kg local potatoes – we use Agria; Maris Piper are good too
2 pieces of white fish fillet, weighing about 180g each – cod, haddock or hake are all good
malt vinegar
sea salt

For the Rockfish batter

195g plain flour
5g baking powder
1g salt
220ml cold water

Heat a deep pan of oil to 145°C. (If you don't have a thermometer or deep-fat fryer, heat the oil in a deep pan – it is hot enough to fry the chips when a small piece of bread dropped in quickly fizzles and crisps.)

Meanwhile, set about peeling the potatoes and cutting them into chips. Blanch the chipped potatoes in batches in the hot oil for about 8 minutes or until slightly soft to the pinch. Lift out of the oil and allow to cool on kitchen paper for about 1 hour.

Make the batter. Combine the flour, baking powder and salt in a mixing bowl and add 150ml of the water. Mix together with a wire balloon whisk. Now the fun starts as you begin to 'stretch' the gluten present in the mix. To do this, keep whisking the batter for a couple of minutes, then allow to rest for a minute. Slowly mix in the rest of the water to form a thin coating batter. Allow to rest for 5–10 minutes before using.

Heat the oil again, now to 175°C. Dry the pieces of fish on kitchen paper. One at a time, holding the fish with your fingertips, dip in the batter to coat and allow excess to run off, then slip into the hot oil. Deep-fry the fish for 5–6 minutes or until crisp. Drain on kitchen paper.

Deep-fry the chips in the same oil in batches for 2–3 minutes or until crisp. Drain on kitchen paper, season with sea salt and malt vinegar and serve hot with the fish.

THE MARINE STEWARDSHIP COUNCIL (MSC)

When we first opened Rockfish, I was acutely aware that I wasn't going to be able to buy my cod locally, as we aren't a cod fishery this far south and they like ice cold water. Sustainability is a big thing for me so I took myself off to visit Norway and see how they catch and look after their seafood there. It was a pretty amazing trip of discovery, and the Norwegians are really in touch with nature and its balance. The methods of fishing were superb and the processing on board the fishing boats was really state of the art, allowing sustainable fishing from one the most inhospitable areas of ocean in the world.

The fishing grounds have been certified as sustainable to The Marine Stewardship Council (MSC) fisheries standard. The MSC are an organisation that work globally with fisherman to study the species they are fishing and ensure they continue to be harvested sustainably. For me they are important in preserving our oceans for the future.

It's not just overseas fisheries that are working with them. A Cornish hake fishery has had certification for several years now and is a real British success story. I know that this initiative is being considered for other species too, which would be a fabulous achievement for our own fisheries.

FRIED SCAMPI
with whisky mayonnaise

You can't beat a bowl of fried scampi. Sadly these days most of it is just crumb, so if you want to eat good scampi it's worth preparing it yourself. A good fishmonger will sell frozen peeled langoustine tails that just need thawing. They aren't cheap but they are the real deal. The best langoustines are in Scotland and north east England. If you buy them whole in shell, I think simply boiling them in salted water and eating them while they're warm is the best way. Don't be tempted to try peeling them for this recipe because it will be hard work!

The whisky mayo works well with other things too, like a prawn cocktail. A simple salad is a perfect accompaniment to the delicious scampi.

SERVES 2

a good handful of plain flour
2 eggs, beaten
a good handful of panko
    breadcrumbs
20 peeled langoustine tails
vegetable oil for frying
lemon wedges to serve
salt and freshly ground
    black pepper

For the whisky mayonnaise

100ml mayonnaise – your
    favourite brand or make
    your own (see recipe on
    page 131)
50ml tomato ketchup
a good dash of bourbon or
    Scotch whisky to taste
1 tablespoon finely chopped
    curly parsley
a pinch of cayenne pepper

Make the mayonnaise by mixing together all the ingredients, except the cayenne pepper. Season to taste.

Have 3 shallow bowls/plates in front of you. Put the flour in one, the eggs in another and the breadcrumbs in the third. Using one hand, dip the langoustines one by one in flour, then egg and then breadcrumbs, making sure they have an even coating.

Heat 2.5cm of vegetable oil in a frying pan to 170°C. (If you don't have a thermometer, heat the oil until a small piece of bread dropped in quickly fizzles and crisps.) Fry the langoustines, in small batches, for about 2 minutes or until golden on both sides. Drain on kitchen paper, season and serve with the mayo on the side, sprinkled with the cayenne pepper, and a good wedge of lime.

TEMPURA PRAWNS

Tempura is an art form in Japan. You sit around the cook while they expertly crisp-fry vegetables and seafood in the lightest, crispest batter you can imagine. It really is a pleasure to watch and experience. You will have some dipping sauces and salts to go with each piece. This recipe is by no means trying to be the same, but it is a good recipe and achievable at home. I've used prawns but it also works well with strips of fish and, particularly, scallops. There are a few dipping sauces and sprinkles to choose from below, all worth making.

SERVES 2 AS A STARTER

1 egg
150ml cold sparkling water
75g plain flour
vegetable oil for deep-frying
12 large, raw shell-on prawns

Beat the egg and add the water, then whisk in the flour. Leave to stand for 10 minutes.

Heat a deep pan of oil to 180°C. (If you don't have a thermometer you can test the temperature of the oil by dropping in a small cube of bread: it should brown in 30 seconds.)

Peel the prawns, keeping the tails on. Dip the prawns in the batter, then fry in the hot oil for about 2½ minutes or until crisp. Drain on kitchen paper and serve with dipping sauces.

NAM JIM SAUCE
Nice spicy, sweet and hot sauce (see recipe on page 133).

CORIANDER AND GINGER DIPPING SAUCE
Blend a handful of coriander leaves with a 2.5cm piece of peeled ginger, 1 peeled garlic clove, 1 tablespoon brown sugar, 1 tablespoon fish sauce, 100ml toasted sesame or vegetable oil and the juice of ½ lime.

PONZU
This is a basic Japanese dipping sauce made by mixing 50ml dark soy sauce and 100ml rice vinegar with the juice of 1 lime and a dash of mirin.

SALT AND PEPPER MIX
This is delicious sprinkled over the hot prawns (see recipe on page 133).

ROCKFISH SEAFOOD CHOWDER _____

A well-made seafood chowder is delicious, comforting and very easy. I like mine packed with seafood rather that making a thin creamy soup. I think some haddock is essential to give it that extra punch.

SERVES 4

1kg live mussels
500g live clams
200ml white wine
a sprig of thyme
3 garlic cloves, finely chopped
50g butter
4 carrots, finely chopped
1 large leek, finely chopped
1 celery stick, finely chopped
100g diced smoked pancetta (optional)
2 fresh bay leaves – give them a little tear
400ml double cream
300g finely diced potatoes
200g skinless fish fillet, cut into bite-sized pieces – cod, pollack and monkfish all work well
150g skinless smoked haddock fillet, cut into bite-sized pieces
12 peeled raw king prawns or a handful of small peeled prawns
a handful of chopped parsley
salt and freshly ground black pepper

Wash the mussels in cold water. Scrape off any barnacles attached to the shells and pull off the brown wispy beards, if there. Discard any mussels with broken shells. If any mussels are open, tap them sharply. If they don't close, discard them – they are dead and not edible. Rinse the mussels again, then drain in a colander.

Check that all the clam shells are undamaged and tightly shut (or close when tapped). Rinse under cold running water to remove any grit or sand.

Put the mussels and clams in a pan large enough to hold them comfortably without crowding – it's better if they are spread out rather then being piled on top of each other. Add the white wine, thyme and 1 of the garlic cloves. Crank up the heat, cover and steam until the shells open. Leave to cool, then remove the clams and mussels from their shells, discarding any that haven't opened. Strain the juices and reserve.

Melt the butter in the same pan and add the carrots, leek, celery, remaining garlic, pancetta, if using, and bay leaves. Cook gently until the vegetables are softened. Add the reserved shellfish juice and the cream and bring to a simmer. Add the diced potatoes and simmer for 8–10 minutes or until they start to break down.

Add the raw fish and prawns and cook for 5–6 minutes, then add the mussels and clams to warm through for a few minutes. Finish with plenty of chopped parsley and season to taste.

POOLE CLAM CHOWDER
with fried bread

When we opened our Poole restaurant I went to see the local clam fishermen there and was totally amazed by how artisan the whole process of catching the local clams is. The fishermen are a pretty enterprising bunch and have got MSC certification for their catch, which means their work is respecting the sustainability of the stock. This is something that is really important to me, and to all of us at Rockfish.

Their clams are meaty and have a delicious flavour. I pick small ones for cooking with spaghetti and use larger ones for this simple chowder. If you cannot get clams, make it with mussels and have a mussel chowder.

SERVES 4

1kg live clams
175ml white wine
50g butter
1 small white onion,
    finely chopped
3 garlic cloves, finely chopped
100g smoked bacon, finely
    chopped
75ml dry sherry
1 tablespoon plain flour
300ml milk
300ml double cream
2 large potatoes, peeled and
    cut into small cubes
a handful of chopped
    curly parsley
Tabasco sauce
salt and white pepper

Check that all the clam shells are undamaged and tightly shut (or close when tapped). Rinse under cold running water to remove any grit or sand. Put the clams in a covered pan with the wine, bring quickly to the boil and steam them open for about 2 minutes. Leave to cool, then discard any clams that didn't open. Remove the meat from the shells; reserve the cooking liquid.

Melt the butter in a pan and gently fry the onion and garlic until soft but not coloured. Add the bacon and cook for a further 2–3 minutes. Add the sherry and boil until it has almost all evaporated, then stir in the flour and cook for a few minutes. Slowly stir in the milk and cream, then add the potatoes and cook for 15 minutes or until they are soft.

Add the reserved clam cooking juices and the clams and simmer for a few minutes. Finish with the parsley. Season with Tabasco and white pepper plus salt if needed.

CHILLI SEAFOOD RAMEN

I enjoyed a wonderful tour of Japan a few years ago. As you can imagine, the seafood was fabulous and eaten everywhere. We went on trawlers, to sushi and noodle bars, and to eel restaurants to name a few, and every one of them was a new experience, some very challenging.

Every few days, though, I craved noodles, and we often dived into ramen bars late at night for a bowl of deeply satisfying porky, fatty noodle soup and some cold Kirin beers. On the coast we ate seafood ramen. I came up with this simple go-to recipe for when I have the ramen cravings. It's not a purist recipe but is an easy one that everyone can do!

While I loved the food of Japan, I did become aware of how much seafood was eaten across the country. At the famous Tsukiji fish market over £10m was traded in seafood every day – in four days they would have sold the entire year's landings at Brixham. It makes me think a lot about the pressure we put on our oceans and how really small scale fishing is in UK waters.

SERVES 2

2 tablespoons chicken stock powder – you can buy this from Asian stores; it's much better than stock cubes
a dash of mirin cooking wine
3 garlic cloves, grated
1 tablespoon grated fresh ginger
a dash of light soy sauce
sriracha chilli sauce, to taste
10 raw king prawns, peeled
4 scallops without coral, each cut in half horizontally
6 fresh shiitake or chestnut mushrooms, finely sliced
1 small cleaned squid, cut into rings – about 60g
2 packs instant ramen noodles – about 65g each
100g fresh hand-picked white crab meat (optional)
4 spring onions, finely sliced
a handful of fresh coriander leaves, chopped
1 fresh chilli, finely sliced
2 eggs, soft boiled and peeled

First make the stock, which is where you get all your flavour. Pour 750ml water into a saucepan and bring to a simmer. Add the chicken powder, mirin, garlic, ginger and soy and stir, then continue to simmer for 7–8 minutes. Add sriracha to taste (I like a salty chilli-tasting broth) and season with more soy if needed. Add the prawns, scallops, mushrooms and squid and simmer gently for 3–4 minutes to lightly poach the seafood and mushrooms.

Cook the noodles as per the instructions on the pack. Drain and divide between 2 bowls. Bring the stock and seafood just to a simmer. Add the crab, if using, then ladle over the noodles. Garnish with the spring onions, coriander and chilli, and nestle the eggs where you can against the edge of the bowl.

WHOLE SQUID GRILLED
with nam jim sauce

Squid is usually fried or braised, and both are delicious, but cooked over a fire squid really comes into its own. The best-sized squid for grilling are 150–200g each or smaller. Ask your fishmonger to clean them by pulling the tentacles from the body and washing the inside of the squid to remove all the gut and any sand, but leave the fins and fine membrane on the squid. Wash the tentacles. Dry the squid well, ready for grilling.

The heat of the fire is important. Wait until all the flames have died down and the embers are white and smouldering. If you cannot barbecue, the next best thing is an overhead grill. Just make sure you really heat it up before cooking.

SERVES 2

2 cleaned whole squid,
   150–200g each
olive oil
nam jim sauce (see page 133)
lime wedges to serve
salt

Prepare a charcoal fire in the barbecue, or preheat the grill. Brush the squid with olive oil and season with salt, then grill gently, turning about halfway, until it starts to char on the edges of the fins and tentacles – this will take 7–8 minutes.

Spoon the nam jim sauce liberally over the fish and serve with wedges of lime.

GRILLED FISH

Grilling fish is the epitome of simple cooking, but fish often needs nothing more than that to bring out the best in it. The trick, which is best understood by gaining experience of eating seafood, is to be aware of the differences between species. Larger kilo-sized turbot, for instance, have a very juicy, gelatinous flesh and a hidden joy in the white skin when grilled. You have to cook turbot slowly, but when you do the white skin renders down to become something really wonderful. Dover sole stays robust and firm and takes on the flavour of the fire really well, whilst John Dory bubbles and blisters and the skin tastes wonderfully of seaweed. All of this you will discover on your own seafood journey.

For best results when grilled, I suggest rubbing the fish with olive oil and a little salt then sprinkling it with a few breadcrumbs before cooking: this will add crispy bits and texture and protect the flesh a little. However, don't be tempted to cover it with too many breadcrumbs; it's not a coating you're after. Sometimes with red mullet or mackerel, I'll marinate them in wine or vinegar for 30 minutes first to add a little something else.

CRISPY CHILLI SQUID
or *cuttlefish*

This dish is inspired by one of my favourite Chinese restaurant dishes, crispy chilli beef. There's one place that does it better than anywhere – the Peking restaurant in Bath, or Mr Wong's as we call it. This place has been our favourite family restaurant for years. We dream about their chilli beef and will drive a few hours just to eat it. It isn't something we would serve at Rockfish but it is the type of thing that Kirk and I like to play around with for fun when we think about new menus.

SERVES 3

200g cleaned squid or cuttlefish, cut into thin strips about the thickness of a pencil plus individual tentacles
2 good handfuls of rice flour
vegetable oil for deep-frying

For the sauce
2 tablespoons toasted sesame oil
1 carrot, peeled and cut into matchsticks
¼ white onion, finely sliced
½ celery stick, strings removed and finely sliced
2 tablespoons Chinese black vinegar or rice vinegar
1 tablespoon dark soy sauce
1 teaspoon light soy sauce
1 tablespoon caster sugar
a pinch of dried chilli flakes
1 tablespoon tomato ketchup
1 tablespoon grated fresh ginger
2 garlic cloves, sliced
1 teaspoon cornflour

To garnish
1 spring onion, finely sliced
1 fresh red chilli, sliced

First make the sauce. Heat the sesame oil in a saucepan and fry the carrot, onion and celery until softened. Add the vinegar, soy sauces, sugar, chilli flakes, ketchup, ginger and garlic. At this point taste the sauce – it should be hot, sweet and sour. If not add more sugar or vinegar to achieve this. Mix the cornflour with 4 tablespoons water and stir into the sauce, which should turn thick and sticky. Leave the sauce on the side to keep warm.

Place the squid in a container and cover with water. Put the rice flour in another container beside it. Heat the oil in a deep pan to 170°C. (If you don't have a thermometer or deep-fat fryer, heat the oil in a deep pan – it is hot enough to fry the squid when a small piece of bread dropped in quickly fizzles and crisps.) Remove the squid from the water in batches and dip it in the flour to coat, then slip into the oil to fry until crisp (this doesn't take long, only about 2 minutes). Don't overfill the pan with batches of squid as this will cool the oil temperature too fast. Once fried, drain the squid on kitchen paper.

When all the squid has been fried, add it to the sauce and stir to coat lightly. Sprinkle with the spring onion and chilli and serve with rice.

SOFT HERRING ROES
with fried bread & parsley

I think in every book I've written I have included a recipe for roes – that's how keen I am for people to eat them! They carry a bit of nostalgia for me as my grandmother, Kitty, used to cook them for supper quite often. I guess herring roes were more top of the pops then than they are now.

SERVES 2

1 large slice of bread, cut into cubes
1 tablespoon olive oil
250g soft herring roes
plain flour for dusting
50g salted butter
a dash of Worcestershire sauce

1 tablespoon rinsed salted capers
2 tablespoons finely chopped parsley
salt and freshly ground black pepper

Fry the bread cubes in the olive oil until crisp and golden, then drain.

Dust the roes in flour and season. Melt the butter in a frying pan and, when bubbling, lay in the roes one by one. Turn them after a few minutes, then continue to spoon the hot bubbling butter over the roes until they are golden. Remove from the heat and add the Worcestershire sauce, capers and parsley. Plate up and sprinkle with the fried bread cubes.

FRIED COCKLES
& malt vinegar mayonnaise

Cockles are pretty hard to beat simply covered in vinegar, but we love this version with a delicious crisp batter. They still need the malt vinegar flavour to bring out the best from them, so you can either sprinkle it on or serve the cockles with our malt vinegar mayo.

SERVES 4

vegetable oil for deep-frying
250g cockles out of the shell
   – frozen are fine, just thaw
   before cooking
Rockfish batter (see page 74)
malt vinegar mayo
   (see page 131)

Bring a deep pan of oil to 160°C. (If you don't have a thermometer or deep-fat fryer, heat the oil in a deep pan – it is hot enough when a small piece of bread dropped in quickly fizzles and crisps.)

Dry the cockles on kitchen paper, then coat in the batter and deep-fry in the hot oil for 1–2 minutes or until crisp. If they bunch up in the oil, move them apart with a fork. Remove from the oil and drain on kitchen paper. Dip the cockles into the mayonnaise and enjoy.

FISH BAKED IN SEA SALT

When you bake a fish in salt you create a sealed oven, within the oven, and the flavour that you get is the purest of the species you are cooking. You can pretty much use any fish for this method but my particular favourites are sea bass and bream, or really fresh mackerel or small turbot. The salt you should use is coarse rock salt, which you can get these days from any delicatessen.

When your fish is prepared ask the fishmonger to remove the guts but leave the scales on.

If I do this at home or in our sister restaurant, the Seahorse, we pour 100ml of Pernod over the salt crust and set it alight, then serve it flaming to be broken open at the table. The flambé gives a lovely scent of anise and adds some theatre to a grand but simple way of cooking fish.

SERVES 2

2kg rock salt
1 sea bass or sea bream, weighing 450–600g (gutted weight) – this is a good size for 1 or 2 to share as a light lunch
a few sprigs of rosemary, savory or thyme

Preheat the oven to 180°C Fan/200°C/Gas Mark 6.

Take a roasting tray or ovenproof dish that will hold the fish and make a layer of salt about 12.5mm thick on the bottom. Dry the fish and stuff the belly cavity with some herb sprigs to add flavour, then lay it on the salt. Cover the fish with the remaining salt and sprinkle over some water. Press the salt down to pack it on to the fish. Bake for 25 minutes. During baking the salt will form a firm crust. Remove from the oven and leave to rest for 10 minutes; the fish will continue to cook.

To check if the fish is cooked, you can use a probe thermometer, which should register 63°C; or insert a metal skewer into the middle part of the fish – when removed the skewer should feel hot.

Break the salt crust with the back of a spoon – it should come off in large chunks, revealing the fish. When the fish is exposed, brush the remaining salt from it with a pastry brush. Lift the fish on to a plate and peel back the skin.

Serve beautifully unadorned.

CANNED SARDINES ON TOAST
with capers & red onion

I love canned seafood. It becomes something different in the canning process. Oily fish like tuna, mackerel and sardines are particularly delicious. I have always wanted to can seafood caught in the UK. Canning seems to be something we don't do much in this country yet in ports across Brittany and northern Spain it is quite a craft, and the canned anchovies and tuna from those areas are revered the world over. They're even more expensive than the fresh catch.

There is a healthy sardine fishery in Cornwall. We bought a tonne of the new season's catch in 2019 and worked with a Spanish seafood cannery to have the fish popped into cans. We tasted them alongside the very best of the Portuguese and Spanish rivals and arrived at the conclusion that the Cornish sardines set the bar, being fat, oily and delicious.

I'm often asked what you can do with canned sardines. This is how I prepare them at home, just a simple combination of ingredients. But the sardine mayonnaise we make at the restaurants is what transforms the dish.

SERVES 2

1 x 140g can sardines
   (I recommend Rockfish
   brand or Ortiz)
sardine mayonnaise
   (see page 130)
½ red onion, finely sliced
1 tablespoon capers, rinsed
   and drained
1 tablespoon finely chopped
   curly parsley
1 dill pickle, finely sliced
2 slices of sourdough bread
salt and white pepper

Drain the oil from the can of sardines and use it to make the mayonnaise.

Put the sardines in a bowl with the onion, capers, parsley and pickle. Gently break up the fish but leave nice chunks. Season. Toast the bread, then heap the sardine mixture on top. Serve the mayo on the side.

PIZZA 'CLAMINARA'

There is nothing not to like about this dish and it can be easily made at home. Garlic, crisp bread and a creamy topping of sweet clams. The method was inspired by Pizza Pilgrims, the best pizza guys in London. During the lockdown of 2020 they launched an at-home pizza kit that fascinated me, and I watched their video on how to make a delicious pizza in a frying pan. It was genius and it works! Take the time to make this dish. It's super. If you like folded pizza, just fold it over before cooking and enjoy a 'clamzoni'.

MAKES 4

For the dough
a 7g sachet of fast-action
    dried yeast
500g strong white flour
325ml tepid water
1 tablespoon olive oil
5g salt
5g caster sugar

For the sauce
1kg live clams
100ml white wine
1 bay leaf
1 peperoncini – hot red chilli
20g butter
20g plain flour
200ml milk
2 garlic cloves, grated
a handful of chopped
    curly parsley

To finish
1 tablespoon grated Parmesan
1 mozzarella ball (about 125g),
    roughly torn

Make the dough by mixing together the yeast, flour, water, olive oil, salt and sugar. Knead on a floured surface for about 5 minutes to make a nice elastic dough. Place in a bowl, cover with a tea towel or clingfilm and leave to rise until doubled in size. This will take 1–1½ hours depending on room temperature. Knock the dough back, then divide into 4 portions. Pinch and shape each into a ball and leave under the cover of a towel to prove for 30 minutes.

To make the sauce, prepare the clams. First check that all the shells are undamaged and tightly shut (or close when tapped). Rinse under cold running water to remove any grit or sand, then put the clams in a pan with the wine, bay and chilli. Cover and steam the clams until they open, about 2 minutes. When cooled, remove the clams from their shells, keeping the meat and the liquid; discard the shells and any clams that didn't open as well as the bay leaf and chilli.

Melt the butter in a smaller pan and stir in the flour. Cook for a couple of minutes to make a roux. Mix the clam cooking liquid and the milk together and pour gradually into the roux, stirring or whisking to make a smooth white sauce. Add the garlic and parsley and simmer for 3–4 minutes. The sauce should be creamy and quite thick. Add the clam meat and stir through. Set aside.

Shape each ball of dough into a disc to fit the pan you are going to use. Push up a raised rim all around.

Preheat the grill. Heat your ovenproof frying pan over a high heat and, when hot, place one of the pizza dough discs in it. Spread a quarter of the clam sauce over the pizza, up to the raised rim. Sprinkle with a little Parmesan and dot some mozzarella liberally all over the pizza. Cook for 4–5 minutes or until the bottom of the pizza is crisp and the edges are starting to rise.

Place the pan under the hot grill to finish cooking – the edges will rise and blister and the cheese will melt and brown. Once the pizza looks full of appeal, take it out and serve, then repeat with the remaining pizza dough discs and topping.

FISH CAKES
with romesco sauce

Fishcakes are a good way of using up offcuts of fish, but it is also worth buying fish just to make them. Cheaper cuts like pollock and coley work well, as does a can of tuna or canned sardines if you don't have anything fresh to hand. It's the combination of mash and fish that everyone loves! The romesco sauce recipe is delicious with fishcakes but so is the anchovy mayonnaise on page 130.

MAKES 4 CAKES

400g skinless fish fillets,
    any remaining small
    bones removed
300g mashed potato
1 tablespoon capers,
    roughly chopped
a squeeze of lemon
a small handful of finely
    chopped flat-leaf parsley
3 tablespoons plain flour,
    seasoned with salt and
    pepper, for coating
2 eggs, beaten
2 good handfuls of fine
    dry breadcrumbs –
    panko ideally
vegetable oil for shallow frying
romesco sauce (see page 133)
salt and freshly ground
    black pepper

Preheat the oven to 200°C Fan/220°C/Gas Mark 7. Place the fish on a roasting tray and roast for 8 minutes, then allow to cool.

When cool enough to handle, flake the fish into a bowl. Mix in the mashed potato and chopped capers, together with a squeeze of lemon and the parsley. Season. Divide the mixture into 4 balls, then flatten into rounds. Chill for 30 minutes before coating.

Have 3 shallow bowls/plates in front of you, one with the flour, one with the beaten eggs and one with the breadcrumbs. Dip each fishcake first in flour, then egg and last of all breadcrumbs, making sure that you have an even coating all round.

Shallow fry the fishcakes in a little vegetable oil over a low to medium heat for 5–6 minutes on each side or until golden. Serve hot with the romesco sauce.

MUSSELS
steamed with wine, bay, chilli & parsley

Tucked in the corner of Torbay is Elberry Cove where mussels are grown on ropes. To this day these mussels are the finest we have ever tasted. They are similar to the French Bouchot variety, which are small and thin-shelled, with a silky delicious meat. We don't use cream with our mussels, preferring the amalgamation of butter and oil. The addition of bay leaves is essential – it gives the dish a wonderful savoury edge – while the chilli provides a backdrop of gentle heat.

SERVES 4

2 garlic cloves, finely chopped
1 shallot, finely chopped
2 bay leaves, torn a bit
1 small dried red
   chilli, crushed
olive oil
25g butter
1.2kg prepared mussels
   (see Rockfish Seafood
   Chowder on page 85)
1 tablespoon chopped parsley
a glass of dry white wine

Gently sweat the garlic and shallot with the bay leaves and crushed red chilli in a little olive oil and the butter until softened but not browned. Add the mussels and parsley, and toss together. Add the wine, then cover and boil for 3–4 minutes, giving the pan a shake from time to time. The mussels are ready when they have opened – be sure to discard any that don't. Spoon the mussels and juice into serving bowls.

LYME BAY MUSSELS

Grown at
50,34,02 N
03,14,20 W

Lyme Bay is one of the most beautiful parts of the south coast and is a protected marine reserve.

We work with our friends Nicky and John at Offshore Shellfish who have established a brilliant marine farm growing mussels on ropes. These shellfish are suspended in some of the cleanest water in the UK where they feed on tiny plankton which become their delicious meat.

In the corner of Torbay is Elberry Cove, a wonderful place to dive, swim and wakeboard. Here is a small marine farm which also produces small sweet mussels that I have been a fan of for years.

Mussels are one of the most sustainable seafoods around and they add to the overall health of the ocean's ecosystem. It's a seafood we should definitely be eating more of: they are easy to cook, sustainable, healthy, good for planet earth and wonderfully delicious.

When they are ready, the mussels are harvested by barge and brought back to shore for purification. At certain times of the year, the waters are Grade A and so the mussels can be eaten safely straight from the water.

These wonderful pictures were taken on 28th February 2021, and capture the beautiful environment these mussels are grown in.

HAKE KIEVS

Who doesn't love chicken Kiev? Warm, melting garlic butter with seafood is another match that is hard to beat. I love playing around with the big fryers, so Kirk and I tried these out one day. We loved them and thought they would be popular. We knew that the chefs would hate us for even thinking about putting them on the menu as they are a little fiddly. Easy for two but tough for 200!

SERVES 2

100g garlic butter
  (see page 133)
2 thick portions of skinless
  hake fillet, weighing about
  200g each
2 eggs, beaten
2 handfuls of plain flour
panko breadcrumbs
oil for deep-frying

Make your garlic butter, then shape it into a block about the same length as a pack of butter (that's about 10cm). Wrap in baking parchment and put it in the freezer for 30 minutes to set hard – this ensures that when you cook the fish you'll get the butter oozing out.

Place a fillet portion on a work surface. Place one hand on top of the fillet and, with a sharp knife, make an incision about two-thirds of the way into the fish to make a pocket. Do this with the other portion of fillet. Take the butter from the freezer and cut it in half. Slot a piece of butter into each fish fillet, pushing it well inside.

Put the eggs in a bowl and the flour and breadcrumbs on separate plates. Using one hand, dip each piece of fish first in the flour, then the egg and finally the breadcrumbs. Repeat this 2 or 3 times until you have nice thick, even coat on each piece of fish. Cover and chill for 30 minutes.

Heat the oil in a deep pan to 170°C. (If you don't have a thermometer or deep-fat fryer, heat the oil in a deep pan – it is hot enough to fry the fish when a small piece of bread dropped in quickly fizzles and crisps.)

Deep-fry the fish Kievs for 6–7 minutes until golden and crisp. Alternatively, shallow-fry them for 2 minutes on each side, then transfer to a 180°C Fan/200°C/Gas Mark 6 oven and finish cooking for 5–6 minutes. Serve with a green salad.

SMOKED HADDOCK & EGG HASH

Make this for lunch or brunch. If you want the best smoked haddock on the planet go to alfredenderby.co.uk. It is the best I've ever tasted.

SERVES 2

300ml milk
2 portions of smoked haddock fillet, weighing about 225g in total, skinned
50g butter
200g potatoes, peeled and boiled until tender
10 curry leaves – if you can get them; leave them out if you can't
1 teaspoon mild curry powder
2 tablespoons peas – thawed frozen are fine
3 spring onions, chopped
1 tablespoon chopped chives
2 eggs, poached or fried

Put the milk into a saucepan and bring to a simmer, then add the smoked haddock. Simmer for 7 minutes. Put the lid on the pan and remove from the heat. When the fish has cooled, drain it and discard the milk.

Melt the butter in a frying pan. When bubbling crush the potatoes in your hand, or using a fork, and fry them gently in the butter, with the curry leaves if using, until they are starting to crisp. Add the curry powder.

Flake the fish into the potatoes. Add the peas and then the spring onions and chives, and cook for a few more minutes. Divide between 2 plates and serve with a runny poached egg or a perfectly fried egg on top.

THE SKIPPER'S ROLL

Nick the Fish, as I call him, is the skipper of the Rockfisher. She's a small boat that works a day at a time out of Brixham. I love being there when Nick lands to see what he's got and have a catch up. He loves his fish and we make this roll for him. It is so good it ended up on the menu. You can fry the fish or grill it, and use whatever is in season – bream, mackerel, gurnard, plaice, lemon sole. Spice it up by loading with jalapeño tartare.

SERVES 2

2 fillets of fish – try bream; keep the skin on but ask your fishmonger to remove all the pinbones
olive oil
2 soft white bread rolls
butter

8 slices of cucumber
a handful of finely shredded iceberg lettuce
2 tablespoons jalapeño tartare (see page 130)
salt

Preheat the grill. Rub the fish skin with salt and olive oil, then grill it, skin side up, or fry in a pan with a little oil – don't turn it, just crisp the skin and wait for the heat to cook the fish.

Split open the rolls, butter and then gently toast in a deep frying pan until golden brown. Place the cucumber slices on the bottom of the rolls, then the lettuce and jalapeño tartare, and then the fish on top. Put the lid on and enjoy!

OUR BREAKFAST SCALLOP & BLACK PUDDING ROLL

This was a favourite at our café downstairs in Brixham, both with customers and with fishermen just coming in from the morning market. Macsween's black pudding is what makes this roll so good, being really peppery and perfect with the wonderfully sweet Brixham scallops.

SERVES 2

6 scallops without corals, each cut in half horizontally
melted butter
2 slices Macsween's black pudding
2 soft white bridge-style rolls – or round rolls if you prefer
2 tablespoons tomato ketchup

2 tablespoons mayonnaise – your favourite brand or make your own (see recipe on page 131)
1 tablespoon French's American-style mustard
malt vinegar
a sprinkling of chopped parsley

Preheat the grill. Brush the scallops with a little melted butter. Place the black pudding slices under the grill and grill for about 4 minutes. Add the scallops and grill for a further 1–2 minutes or until cooked. Meanwhile, split the rolls from the top two-thirds of the way down and toast on the inside under the grill. Mash the black pudding down the middle of each roll. Mix the ketchup with the mayo and mustard and spoon down the middle, then top with the scallops. Finish with a drizzle of malt vinegar and a sprinkle of parsley.

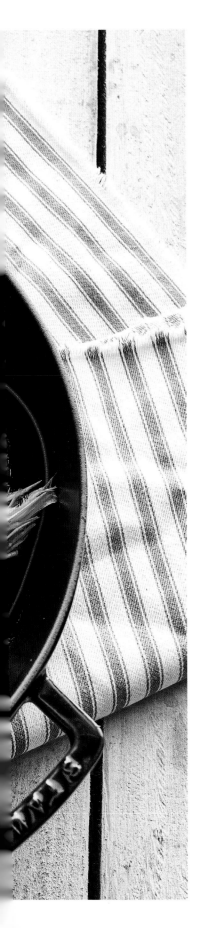

SOUTH COAST FISH STEW

This recipe has been with me ever since I started cooking. It was the first fish stew I ever made – on a beach in Greece somewhere with my then three-year-old son Ben. As we were cooking, an octopus wrapped itself around his foot, scaring the life out of him. We cooked and ate the stew together, sitting with our feet in the water. Later we looked for sea urchins, hanging over rocks to see if we could spot any. He marvelled at finding his first ones. Ben is now a far better chef than I am and I suspect even at that young age he was forming his love of the kitchen.

SERVES 4

olive oil
2 shallots, finely chopped
4 ripe tomatoes, roughly
    chopped
2 garlic cloves, finely chopped
a sprig of thyme
50ml Pernod
a glass of white wine
a pinch of saffron threads
a handful of chopped
    curly parsley
1.5g fish, gutted and cut into
    chunks – gurnard, monkfish
    and red mullet are best (if
    using fillets, cut into bite-
    sized pieces, you'll only
    need 500g)
200g prepared mussels (see
    Rockfish Seafood Chowder
    on page 85)
salt

Heat a little oil in a large saucepan and fry the shallots until softened. Add the tomatoes, garlic and thyme. When the tomatoes are softening add the Pernod and set alight. When the flames die down, add the wine and boil until almost all evaporated.

Add the saffron and parsley. Pour in about 600ml water and add a good pinch of salt. Bring to a simmer. Add the fish and mussels, cover and simmer for 4–5 minutes or until the fish is cooked and the mussels have opened. Season – it may take a lot of salt but you will find the balance. Think sea water.

MY FAVOURITE FISH CURRY
with fried parathas

I love a fish curry. I particularly like fish head curry, which is delicious. I first ate it at a restaurant in Singapore called Sammy's, where they serve wonderful fragrant pots of curry that are so richly flavoured from the slow simmering of the fish head with spices and aromatics. If you feel brave and can get hold of a few bass, bream or salmon heads it's worth having a go, using the sauce recipe below. For fish curries use firm-fleshed fish like gurnard, monkfish or mackerel, which are delicious cut into chunks or left on the bone, if you like to eat fish this way.

I serve this with fried parathas. I first had them when working with my friend Mark Hix, who was serving them as a starter at one of the Pig's smoked and uncut festivals. Parathas are usually cooked in a pan but frying them is something truly wonderful.

SERVES 4

4 garlic cloves, chopped
1 onion, roughly chopped
a 5cm knob of fresh ginger, peeled and chopped
vegetable oil for frying
20 curry leaves – fresh are best
a pinch of fenugreek seeds
1 teaspoon black mustard seeds
½ teaspoon caster sugar
1 tablespoon curry powder
½ teaspoon ground coriander
1 teaspoon ground cumin
½ teaspoon freshly ground black pepper
¼ teaspoon chilli powder
¼ teaspoon ground turmeric
200ml canned coconut milk
1 tablespoon tamarind paste
1 lemongrass stick, bruised with a rolling pin
500g skinless fish fillet, cut into bite-size pieces
2 tomatoes, chopped
2 fresh red chillies, sliced
a good handful of coriander leaves, chopped
frozen parathas to serve
salt

Put the garlic, onion and ginger in a small food processor and blitz to make a paste.

In a pan large enough to take the fish heat a few teaspoons of oil. When it is hot add the curry leaves and fenugreek and mustard seeds. Fry until they crackle, then add the onion paste and fry together for a few minutes, stirring. Add the sugar and the rest of the spices, then cook, stirring, until the raw smell of spices is gone. Add 250ml water followed by the coconut milk and then the tamarind and lemongrass. Stir well. Simmer gently for 20 minutes.

Season to taste. Add the fish and simmer gently for a further 4 minutes or until it is cooked. Stir in the tomatoes and sliced chillies, then sprinkle with coriander and it's ready to serve.

To cook the parathas, heat a deep pan of oil to 170°C. Cut the frozen parathas into quarters and drop 2 pieces at a time into the hot oil. Fry until crispy – they will puff up and have golden brown layers. Drain on kitchen paper and serve with the curry.

FRIED SCALLOPS
with malt vinegar & jalapeño tartare _____

This is the ultimate fried seafood. If you're up for deep-frying at home this is pretty easy to do, and much simpler than frying a piece of fish for fish and chips.

Fresh scallops are usually easy to come across but if you're finding it difficult, look in your supermarket freezer. I came across some brilliant scallops from Canada, the Clearwater brand. Normally I would say to avoid frozen scallops but for this dish they are fine. The Canadian scallops were a really good size and not full of water, but what really made it for me was that they are MSC-certified. This is a standard all fisheries should work towards and gives us confidence that what we are eating is truly sustainable, which is as important as being local. So don't shy away from properly harvested sustainable seafood coming from another country.

SERVES 2

6 tablespoons cornflour
6 tablespoons plain flour
ice-cold sparkling water
1 quantity jalapeño tartare
   (see page 130)
malt vinegar
vegetable oil for deep-frying
12 scallops without coral, each
   cut in half horizontally
lemon wedges to serve
sea salt

First make your batter by mixing the flours and adding enough sparkling water to make a double cream consistency.

Blitz the tartare sauce so that is smooth (this makes dipping easy, but leave it chunky if you prefer). Season with plenty of malt vinegar – you want the sauce sharp to cut through the batter.

Heat your oil to 170°C. (If you don't have a thermometer or deep-fat fryer, heat the oil in a deep pan – it is hot enough to fry the scallops when a small piece of bread dropped in quickly fizzles and crisps.) Dip the discs of scallop in the batter and fry a few at a time for 3–4 minutes or until crisp. Don't put too many scallops into the pan or the oil temperature will fall and your scallops will be soggy. Drain on kitchen paper. When all the scallops are cooked sprinkle with a little sea salt and serve with the sauce for dipping and lemon wedges for squeezing.

ROASTED SCALLOPS
with white wine & garlic

This was a dish we first cooked at the Seahorse 12 years ago and it has never left the menu. It also found its way on to the Rockfish menu about five years ago and is now a firm favourite here too. The only difference between them is that we use white port instead of wine at the Seahorse and cook the scallops in a charcoal oven. Both versions are delicious. Rockfish guests say the dish is better at Rockfish and the Seahorse guests say it is better at the Seahorse – they are virtually the same!

SERVES 2

6 scallops in the half shell
6 tablespoons white wine
50g garlic butter (see page 133)
6 tablespoons fresh
    breadcrumbs
6 tablespoons olive oil

Preheat the oven to 220–240°C Fan/240°C/Gas Mark 9 or its highest setting. You need plenty of heat. Cut a piece of foil twice the length of your roasting tray, then scrunch it up to fit into the tray – this gives you a stable base on which to sit the scallops.

Place the scallops in their half shells on the foil and press down so they are firmly held. Add 1 tablespoon of white wine to each shell, then place a tablespoon of garlic butter on each one. Sprinkle with breadcrumbs and finish with a drizzle of olive oil.

Roast for 5–7 minutes or until bubbling – the butter should have melted and the breadcrumbs absorbed most of it, creating a slushy, garlicky, winey sauce crisped by the oven heat.

SEA BREAM BAKED IN PAPER
with garlic, olive oil, chilli & rosemary

Cooking a fish 'en papillote', or in a bag, is an excellent way to prepare it. The fish retains its moistness and the other flavours that you add really get a chance to develop with the flavours of the fish to create something quite magical. The combination of roasted garlic, chilli and rosemary is a good one, as is thyme, lemon and cumin. But you will find your own preferences.

Look for wild gilt head or black bream, or use farmed gilt head bream, which are delicious and perfectly acceptable. Ask your fishmonger to scale and gut the fish and remove the head.

SERVES 2

8 garlic cloves
100ml olive oil
2 whole sea bream,
    weighing about 450g
    each, head removed
1 small fresh bird's eye chilli,
    finely sliced
4 sprigs of rosemary
50ml white wine
finely chopped parsley
salt

Preheat the oven to 160°C Fan/180°C/Gas Mark 4.

Place your garlic cloves, with the skin on, on a small roasting tray, drizzle with a little of the olive oil and sprinkle with some salt. Roast for 10 minutes or until soft – you should be able to squeeze the garlic from the skin. If not then just cook a little longer. Set aside to cool slightly.

Turn up the oven to its maximum heat.

Cut out 2 pieces of baking parchment large enough to enclose a fish. Lay the parchment on the worktop and place the fish on it. Sprinkle the chilli over the fish and place the peeled garlic around it. Tuck some rosemary into the belly. Sprinkle with salt and pour over the rest of the olive oil. Fold the paper up and over the fish, and just before you seal it up completely, pour the wine into the corner, then finish sealing.

Place the parchment bags on a baking tray and cook for 15 minutes. Cut the paper open, sprinkle the fish with chopped parley and serve straight from the bag.

SAUCES & SIDES

OUR FAVOURITE SAUCES

As we keep saying, a good piece of fish doesn't need much. It just needs to be fresh and properly cooked. But a dipping sauce with some heat or acidity can really bring out the best in a piece of fish. It's like the magic that happens to chips when you add the salt and vinegar.

The first few sauces here are mayonnaise-based. Apart from the anchovy mayonnaise and sardine mayonnaise, you can easily make the others just by adding a few extra ingredients to a basic mayonnaise. I often make my own mayo at home but when the restaurants are very busy we have to use a commercial brand (our favourite is a vegan mayonnaise as we find it more creamy). So don't feel bad about taking your favourite shop-bought mayo and adding to it.

Rockfish tartare
SERVES 4

Add 80g chopped dill pickles, 20g capers, 25g chopped red onion and some chopped curly parsley and dill to 125g mayo.

Jalapeño tartare
SERVES 4

Add as many finely chopped pickled jalapeños to the Rockfish tartare recipe as you can stand.

Seaweed tartare
SERVES 4

Add 1 tablespoon mixed fine seaweed flakes that have been steeped in malt vinegar for 5 minutes to rehydrate plus some grated lemon zest to Rockfish tartare.

Marie Rose sauce
SERVES 4

Mix 60/40 mayo and ketchup. Add a good glug of dry sherry or brandy, a dash of Worcestershire sauce and plenty of Tabasco.

Sardine mayo
SERVES 2

Whisk 1 egg yolk with 1 teaspoon Dijon mustard and 1 tablespoon tomato paste. Drain the oil from a 140g can of sardines and slowly drizzle it into the yolk mixture while whisking to build up a nice thick mayonnaise. Season and add a splash of Tabasco or other chilli sauce to taste.

Anchovy mayo
SERVES 4

Blend together 40g anchovies, 2 egg yolks, 10g balsamic vinegar, 10g Dijon mustard, 10g capers and 10g chopped parsley until smooth. Slowly incorporate 200ml vegetable oil, or vegetable oil mixed with oil from the can of anchovies, until you reach the desired consistency, just as if making a regular mayonnaise.

Mayonnaise
SERVES 4

This makes about 400ml. Whisk together 2 egg yolks, 1 tablespoon Dijon or English mustard, a dash of white wine vinegar and a pinch of salt. Continue to whisk while you drizzle in 250ml vegetable oil in a steady stream until you have a thick, creamy mayonnaise. Taste and add more vinegar if needed. Season.

Quick sardine mayo
SERVES 4

This is a quick version of the sardine mayo recipe on page 130. Add a few tablespoons of oil from a can of sardines to 75g mayo, or to taste, plus a pinch of cayenne pepper and 1 tablespoon tomato paste. Mix together.

Gherkin vinegar mayo
SERVES 4

Add a good glug of vinegar and a few spices from a jar of dill pickles to a few tablespoons of mayo plus a good pinch of white pepper.

Lemon mayo
SERVES 4

Replace the vinegar with lemon juice.

Malt vinegar mayo
SERVES 4

Add a good glug of brown malt vinegar plus a good pinch each of white pepper and salt to a few tablespoons of mayo. This is amazing with fried fish.

Hot chilli, lime & coriander mayo
SERVES 4

Blitz the juice of 2 limes with a little caster sugar and a handful of fresh coriander. Mix into 125ml mayo with a good squeeze of sriracha chilli sauce.

Mojo verde mayo
SERVES 4

Blitz together a handful of fresh coriander, a handful of parsley, 1 garlic clove, 1 teaspoon ground cumin, juice of 2 limes, a pinch of white pepper and some salt with 100g mayo. This is super with grilled fish.

The idea is crunch, freshness and mixed textures. To get the best out of this, slice or chop everything nice and fine.

SERVES 4

a bunch of spring onions, sliced
   on the bias
½ cucumber, peeled, deseeded
   and thinly sliced
1 green pepper, peeled and
   finely chopped
1 tablespoon chopped capers
1 tablespoon chopped gherkin
1 tablespoon finely sliced
   green olives

1 tablespoon chopped mixed
   herbs (tarragon, mint,
   parsley and chives)
75ml olive oil
lemon juice
agrodolce or muscatel vinegar
salt

Combine the spring onion, cucumber, green pepper, capers, gherkin, olives and herbs in a bowl, and mix loosely with the olive oil. Balance the flavour with lemon juice, agrodolce or moscatel vinegar and salt.

Nam jim sauce
SERVES 4

Put a small handful each of coriander leaves and Vietnamese mint leaves (or English mint if you cannot find Vietnamese) in a mortar and pestle with a 2.5cm piece of fresh ginger, finely grated, 2 peeled garlic cloves, 2 fresh red chillies, finely chopped, and a pinch of coarse salt. Crush and pound to a paste. Throw in 1 finely chopped shallot and crush a little more. Add 2 tablespoons fish sauce, the juice of 1 lime and 2 tablespoons palm sugar, or to taste, and mix in. Balance the flavours by adding more of any of these ingredients. You want a sauce that is salty, sweet and hot.

Singapore-style chilli sauce
SERVES 4

Mix together 6 tablespoons sweet chilli sauce, 1 tablespoon kecap manis, ½ teaspoon grated fresh ginger and a dash of fish sauce.

Sauce mignonette
SERVES 4

This is great for dressing fresh oysters or for eating with cold steamed shellfish. Simply take 6 tablespoons red wine vinegar and mix with 2 very finely chopped shallots, then season with plenty of freshly ground black pepper.

Romesco sauce
SERVES 4

Soak 4 dried ñora or choricero chillies to rehydrate, then remove seeds. Put into a food processor with 100g whole blanched almonds and pulse until roughly chopped. Add 6 peeled garlic cloves, 12 roasted piquillo peppers (or 6 roasted and peeled sweet peppers), 1 teaspoon each sweet paprika and smoked paprika plus ¼ teaspoon hot smoked paprika. Pulse to combine. Add 25ml sherry vinegar, 100ml olive oil and a pinch of salt, and pulse again to produce a thick sauce that is neither too chunky nor too smooth.

Dill pickle relish
SERVES 4

Put a few dill pickles, ¼ onion, a few capers, some chopped parsley and a good few tablespoons of piccalilli in a blender and pulse. Great with all grilled seafood.

Garlic butter
SERVES 4

Soften 125g salted butter at room temperature for 30 minutes before using. Put 4 peeled garlic cloves, a good handful of flat-leaf parsley and 2 salted anchovy fillets into a food processor and pulse to purée. Add the softened butter and blitz for 2–3 minutes, stopping and scraping round the sides a couple of times. Add a splash of Pernod and a couple of drops of Tabasco or other chilli sauce.

Salt & pepper mix
SERVES 4

Put equal amounts of pink, white, black and Sichuan peppercorns in a pestle with the same quantity of sea salt flakes and give them all a good bash about until they are coarsely ground. Store in an airtight jar and use for tossing freshly fried crispy squid or prawns in.

MRS SANDHU'S CURRY SAUCE

You can't beat curry sauce and chips but it has to be the right curry sauce – thick but not gloopy, spicy but not hot, sweet but not overly. It's a thing to get it right. One of my great friends, Nick Sandhu, who works with us at Rockfish, very kindly gave me a container or two of his mum's home-made curries. He had often talked about how good they are, and with me being a cook she thought I might like to taste them. I can only say they were out of this world. That's the thing about cookery – if you understand what you are cooking you have a real connection with it, and Mrs Sandhu made the best curry I had ever eaten. So I asked Nick for his mum's curry sauce recipe and this is what we base ours on at Rockfish. We call it Mr Sandhu's curry sauce on the menu, but we all really know where it came from. This is exactly as she handed down the recipe to us for which we are eternally grateful.

MAKES ABOUT 500ML

1 teaspoon ground cumin
1 tablespoon chopped garlic
1 tablespoon chopped ginger
1 cup of onion, roughly
    chopped (about 150g)
1 stick of celery, roughly
    chopped
3 tablespoons oil
1 teaspoon salt
½ teaspoon ground coriander
½ teaspoon red chilli powder
½ teaspoon turmeric
2 tablespoons curry powder
    of choice
1 tablespoon vegetable
    gravy granules
1½ teaspoons mustard,
    wholegrain
1 tablespoon tomato paste
2 tablespoons cornflour
2 tablespoons milk
butter

Sauté ½ teaspoon of the cumin, the garlic, ginger, onion and celery in the oil until light brown.

Mix the remaining ½ teaspoon of cumin with the salt, coriander, chilli powder, turmeric, curry powder, gravy granules, mustard, tomato paste and ⅓ cup (80ml) water, before adding to the sautéed ingredients. Cook for 5 minutes until combined well.

Then add 2 cups (500ml) water and simmer for 5 minutes until everything is well combined. Take off the heat. Cool and blend using a hand blender until a smooth consistency is formed.

In a bowl, mix the cornflour and milk with 3 tablespoons water until smooth.

Add the cornflour mixture to the sauce with a knob of butter and cook on a low heat until sauce is thickened. Adjust the seasoning to taste.

That's it – the best curry sauce on the planet!

SIDES

Keep these simple – it's often the easiest and simplest dishes that work best of all. For example, you cannot beat a Greek salad with anything from the sea! Here are some of our favourites.

Greek salad
SERVES 2

Roughly chop some tomatoes and cucumber. Slice some green peppers and red onions. Make a dressing from good red wine vinegar, a pinch of sugar and good olive oil. Add plenty of dried oregano and whisk together. Toss the salad vegetables together and dress. Place in a bowl and break salty feta over the top. Finish with more oregano and a drizzle of olive oil.

Pickled chilli slaw
SERVES 2

Shred some white cabbage and a few dill pickles on a mandoline – you want the pickles to be in matchsticks the length of the pickle. Do the same with some carrot. Finely chop a bunch of spring onions and slice 4 green chillies (or use pickled jalapeños). Toss everything in a little of the vinegar from the dill pickle jar, then mix in a few tablespoons of mayo to bring it all together.

Little Gems, salad cream & anchovies
SERVES 2

This is just that. Take the outer leaves off the lettuce – you want the sweet hearts – and quarter them. Lay them side by side on a plate. Season, then spoon a tablespoon or two of salad cream on to each one and top with a salted anchovy.

Jersey Royals & seaweed butter
SERVES 2

I love the first new potato crop of the year. Jersey Royals are grown in soil covered in seaweed to enrich it, so this is a fitting dish for them. Simply boil your potatoes, then mix plenty of butter with a few tablespoons of the cooking water until melted. Add a few tablespoons of dried fine flakes of seaweed and plenty of salt. Pour into a serving bowl and place the potatoes in it so you can scoop them out with plenty of butter.

Pickled veg
SERVES 2

I like to pickle my own veg at home but the restaurants are so busy that we look out for the best commercial pickles and serve those. Fish and pickles are a match made in heaven and in all cuisines you will find something interesting. Here are a few of the things we like to serve alongside fish: malt vinegar onions; dill pickles; cornichons; caper berries; pickled jalapeños; balsamic onions; pickled guindillas – the sweet-sour Spanish chillies; pickled fennel; piccalilli – with the Smoked Haddock and Egg Hash on page 112.

Fried pickles _____

SERVES 2

Pretty indulgent but just grab a handful of pickles – dills, guindillas or whatever you fancy – dip them in the Rockfish batter (see page 74) and deep-fry until crisp.

Crispy samphire fritters

SERVES 2

This is a great way to serve samphire, although I do like it just boiled to suck off the stems with plenty of butter too. Mix 100g gram flour with a little water to make a thick batter. Add a pinch each of English mustard powder, ground cumin and salt plus a splash of vinegar, then a handful each of sliced onion and samphire. Mix together with your hand. Shallow-fry in half-handful-sized clumps until crisp, then serve with a wedge of lemon and a sprinkle of dill.

Curried mushy peas

SERVES 2

This now-famous dish was invented at Rockfish Brixham on a morning when I needed a curry fix! I grabbed a pot of mushy peas, topped them with Mrs Sandhu's Curry Sauce (see page 135), sprinkled over some fresh coriander and sliced red onion, and that was it. The dish made it on to the menu a week later and we have been serving it for the last 5 years. A simple Rockfish classic!

ACKNOWLEDGEMENTS

There are so many people I would like to thank. Firstly, to every single person who has been part of Rockfish during this extraordinary 2020 year – thanks for your loyalty and support for what we do, you're an amazing bunch.

Thanks to Laura Cowan for getting this book off the ground: you made it happen. Kirk Gosden for the brilliant energy you bring, and for being my wingman on this book. Mat Prowse, you've been on this journey with me for years, my very dear friend, and there's no stopping yet, Jeff! Jon Croft, who I love producing books with, and Meg, Em, Marie and all the publishing team. Chris Terry, doing books with you is always great – you're a top man. Ed Ovenden, thanks for your magnificent talent, you're a star. There isn't the space to thank the many other people who have been part of the Rockfish story, but you know who you are, thank you.

Huge thank you to my son Ben (Terry) Tonks and my cousin 'Southside Jeffries' for putting together the Rockfish cookbook playlist on page 11.

And lastly, to my wonderful wife Nellie and our children, Sadie, Ben, Izzy, Blue and Fran, who are all a source of absolute joy and inspiration.

Best fishes!

INDEX

Tina Parratt

Florence

CeDavs

Daisy

Teddchapm   T

H. Tasker.

Harry B

Gibson

Dimi \
S

Mandrell

Ian Parratt

J. Gosden

J. Tastra

JC Tracker

Jonno

Laura Carter

S. Lyddiatt

Scott Kelly

M. Bartho

Louis chapman

M Davis